A PHOTOGRAPHIC GUIDE TO
BIRDS
OF EAST AFRICA

Published by Struik Nature
(an imprint of Random House Struik (Pty) Ltd)
Reg. No. 1966/003153/07
80 McKenzie Street, Cape Town, 8001 South Africa
PO Box 1144, Cape Town, 8000 South Africa

Visit us at **www.randomstruik.co.za**
Log on to our photographic website
www.imagesofafrica.co.za
for an African experience

First published in the UK in 1995 by
New Holland (Publishers) Ltd
24 Nutford Place
London
W1H 6DQ
United Kingdom

Second edition 2000 by Struik Publishers
Third edition 2006 by Struik Publishers

5 7 9 10 8 6 4

Editor: Pippa Parker
Design Manager: Petal Palmer
Designer: Dean Pollard
Cartographer: Lyndall du Toit

Reproduction by Hirt & Carter Cape (Pty) Ltd
Printed and bound by Times Offset (M) Sdn Bhd

ISBN 978 1 77007 381 4

Front cover photograph: Saddle-billed Stork (D Richards)
Title page photograph: Black-shouldered Kite (D Richards)
Back cover photograph: Cinnamon-breasted Bee-eaters (D Richards)

Contents

Introduction

Birdwatching, or birding as it is often called, is an absorbing pas-
time, ever increasing in popularity. In fact, it is now considered to be
one of the major 'sports' in the USA. Few visitors to East Africa can
fail to be impressed by the large variety of colourful birds they see
and by their relative tameness. The region is renowned for its wealth
of wildlife and for the huge diversity of habitats in the regions, these
ranging from snow-covered mountain peaks, deserts and forests
to beautiful golden beaches. The birdlife is even more impressive.
Some 1 388 species have been recorded, which represents approxim-
ately 15 per cent of the world's total. This figure is changing each
year as new bird species are discovered, particularly in Tanzania.
Recent discoveries include a sunbird, a weaver, a cisticola and a
forest partridge whose closest relative is the hill partridge of Asia.
Even though the number of species is slowly increasing, we cannot
afford to be complacent; the destruction of habitat, due largely to an
ever-increasing human population, has placed a number of bird species in danger. The forests of Kakamega, Nandi, Sokoke, Uluguru
and Usambara are all vulnerable. Many birds are threatened, including the Crowned Crane – Uganda's national bird – which is at risk
because of the draining of its swamp habitat and also because of the
trade in wild exotic birds.

This book represents 265 out of the 1 350 species found in East
Africa. Selecting birds for inclusion in this guide was a particularly
difficult task, and preference was given to those species that are
easily seen and to those that occur in areas visited by tourists. This
explains why the Rufous-tailed Weaver and the Long-tailed Widowbird are included even though each occurs in one East African
country only, and in a relatively small area within those countries.
Visitors to Ngorongoro Crater and the Serengeti cannot fail to see
Rufous-tailed Weavers, which are highly gregarious and very noisy
birds. At Narba Hill – the entrance to the Serengeti National Park
– the birds are ever present. The Long-tailed Widow, on the other
hand, occurs only in Kenya and becomes very obvious during the
breeding season to visitors driving between Mount Kenya and the
Aberdares. Those on their way to the Samburu and Buffalo Springs
national reserves are almost sure to see these birds.

If any country has been neglected in this book, it is Uganda. After
years of turmoil it is becoming more stable and friendly, however,
the birders, although in much smaller numbers compared to those
entering Kenya and Tanzania, are again visiting that country. Most
of the birds likely to be seen by visitors to Uganda have been included in this guide.

Field Equipment

Although a number of birds can be seen at close range in the vicinity of safari lodges and hotels, many are furtive or not readily seen
in this context. Because of this, a pair of binoculars is a must when
watching birds. The most popular sizes for birdwatching are 7 x 35
or 8 x 40, both of which are generally small in size and reasonably
light in weight. The first number (7/8) represents the magnification,
and the second (35/40) refers to the diameter of the front lens in
millimetres. Generally, the larger the diameter of the front lens
in relation to the size of the eye-piece lens, the greater the amount
of light gathered and, therefore, the brighter and clearer the image.
Really keen birders often use a 10 x 40 or 10 x 50 combination, but
these tend to be heavy and cumbersome, and are also difficult to
hold steady. Telescopes are becoming increasingly popular in bird-

watching and, if you can cope with the inconvenience of carrying one, can be very useful in identifying distant or very small birds.

Always take a notepad and pencil on any birdwatching expedition: there are certain to be birds you do not recognise, and usually there is not time to page through field guides in an attempt to identify a species. When you do come upon an unknown species, take note of the following features, which will serve as a guide to identify the bird at a later time.

Colour Note the general colour both above and below, as well as any distinctive markings or colouring on the body, wings or tail. Eye colour is also often important, but remember that light can play tricks and may affect colour.

Size and shape Gauge the size of the bird by comparing it with another species with which you are familiar (preferably one nearby). Observe whether it has a long or a short tail.

Bill shape Is it long and thin (as in a sunbird) or short and stout (as in a sparrow)? Bill colour may also be diagnostic.

Legs Are they long or short? Colour again may be important and is worth noting.

Habitat What is the habitat type in which you are viewing the bird: grassland, forest, river or lake, or is it in a garden? Is the bird in a tree or in a bush near to the ground?

Finally, make a note of any characteristic behaviour. What is the bird doing? Is it flying, feeding, hopping, walking, perched or singing? If flying, note the pattern: is it swallow-like or sparrow-like? Is it gliding or hovering. Write down the date, time and place, and perhaps the weather in which you saw the bird.

When birdwatching, try to be as silent as possible, avoid sudden movement and pointing and, if possible, wear dull-coloured clothing rather than white or bright colours.

How to use this book

This book has been designed as a quick and easy-to-use reference in the field. The entries are concise and highlight (in the italic type) the most important or distinctive characteristics of each species. Both common and scientific names are included, which are followed by the letters K, T, and U (or combinations of these), representing Kenya, Tanzania and Uganda respectively and hence indicating the countries in which the bird occurs. The length of the bird (the average length from tip of bill to end of tail) is also given. Distribution maps appearing alongside each species entry show at a glance the areas in which the bird occurs.

Photographs have been selected to show the characteristic features of each bird, and where plumage differences between breeding and non-breeding birds, male and female, or adult and immature birds is marked, this has in most cases been illustrated. Thumbnail silhouettes are intended as a guide to the different bird families as you flick through the pages.

A habitat map depicting the different vegetation zones that characterise the region appears at the back of the book, along with a glossary of terms and a labelled diagram of a bird. Alternative common names appear in the index.

Abbreviations

K = Kenya	T = Tanzania	U = Uganda
cm = centimetres	m = metres	

D. Richards

Male

Males have a black body with contrasting white wings and tail, which are often stained brown. The neck and legs are pink-grey, which turn bright pink in the breeding season. Females and immature are grey-brown. Usually found in dry open plains and lightly wooded grassland.

Somali Ostrich *Struthio molybdophanes* **K 2 – 2,5 m**

Males differ from Common Ostrich by having distinctive blue-grey neck and legs, which become brighter in the breeding season. At this time, the bill and the front of the lower legs become bright pink. Females and immature similar to Common Ostrich. Usually found in more arid areas of north and north-east Kenya. Both Common and Somali are the same size. The Somali Ostrich only occurs in Kenya.)

D. Richards

Male

Little Grebe *Tachybaptus ruficollis* **KTU 20 – 25 cm**

Breeding adult   *Non-breeding adult*

A small, stout, short-necked, and seemingly tailless waterbird. Sexes are alike, having grey-brown upperparts and lighter underparts. The bill is short with a *distinctive pale spot* at its base. When breeding the neck and cheeks turn bright rufous, and the throat and face turn black. The bird dives regularly and also runs along the surface of the water. The call is a distinctive, loud, slightly descending, ringing trill. Found on most fresh-water lakes, dams and ponds in the region.

Great White Pelican *Pelecanus onocrotalus* **KTU 180 cm**

Adults   *Immature*

A large gregarious *all-white* bird. Sexes are similar, showing a blue-pink bill with a red nail at the tip, a yellow pouch, bare pink skin around the eyes, and yellow feet. The *feathers on the head meet in a sharp point above the bill*. Breeding birds are tinged pink and develop swollen knobs at the base of the bill. In the male this knob turns yellow and in the female bright orange, but in both it becomes pink once the eggs are laid. Juvenile and immature are dark brown becoming paler with age, with a grey to black bill, a dark pouch and grey-yellow feet. Found in groups, resting on the shores of soda lakes, and often seen performing their characteristic group-synchronised fishing. They *roost and nest on the ground*, and fly and soar in V-formation when the distinctive *black flight feathers* can be seen.

Pink-backed Pelican *Pelecanus rufescens* **KTU 140 cm**

Adults

Adults in flight

A *greyish* pelican, smaller than the Great White Pelican (p. 7) and found in much smaller groups. Sexes are alike. The back and rump are tinged pink, (seen when bird is preening), the bill is grey-pink with an orange nail at the tip, the pouch and bare skin around the eyes are flesh-coloured, and the feet are yellow. The *feathers on the head form a broad arc above the bill*. Breeding birds develop a grey crest, the pouch turns bright yellow, the feet orange-red and the area around the eyes turns black above and yellow below. Immature is brown with a pale head, a grey bill, a yellow-green pouch and grey-pink skin around the eyes. Feeds alone or in small groups on freshwater lakes. *Roosts and nests in trees.*

Long-tailed Cormorant *Phalacrocorax africanus* **KTU 56 cm**

Adult

Immature

A small, long-tailed cormorant with a short neck and a short bill. Seen singly or in small groups, often perched on a branch overhanging water. Swims low in the water, often with only the head showing. Adult is glossy black with paler wings, *distinctive red eyes and a short stiff crest on the forehead*. Immature and non-breeding birds are brownish to dull black, often paler on the throat, and with brown eyes. Found on lakes, swamps, rivers, dams and mangrove creeks.

8

Great Cormorant *Phalacrocorax carbo* **KTU 90 cm**

Immature

Adult

Larger than the Long-tailed Cormorant and with a *noticeably shorter tail*. Usually occurs in larger numbers, commonly along the shore but roosts in trees. Has a strongly hook-tipped bill. The *eyes are emerald* and the lores are orange in males and scarlet in females. Breeding bird is glossy black with cheeks, throat and upper breast white, and often a *distinctive white patch on the sides of the rump*. Immature is brownish and whitish below. Found on lakes, dams and rivers.

Grey Heron *Ardea cinerea* **KTU 100 cm**

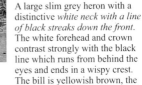

Immature

Adult

A large slim grey heron with a distinctive *white neck with a line of black streaks down the front*. The white forehead and crown contrast strongly with the black line which runs from behind the eyes and ends in a wispy crest. The bill is yellowish brown, the

eyes yellow and the legs brown. Breeding birds have orange-red eyes and reddish legs. In flight the head and neck are tightly tucked in, as in all herons, and the underwings are seen to be entirely grey. Sexes are similar, and immature is paler than adult and has a grey crown. Usually solitary, occurring on lakes, swamps and ponds, and along rivers. Very few nest sites are known, leading ornithologists to believe that the majority these birds breed elsewhere in Africa.

Goliath Heron *Ardea goliath* KTU 140 – 152 cm

Adult

This is the world's largest heron. The *bushy crest on top of the crown and the large heavy bill* are distinctive. The upperparts are slate-grey, and the head, neck and underparts are rich chestnut in colour. The chin and throat are white, and the neck is white with some black streaking. Sexes are alike and immature is generally paler than the adults. The call is a distinctive 'karrrk'. Occurs singly, or in pairs, on lakes, swamps, and along rivers and also coastal creeks. Usually nests solitarily, deep in reedbeds and just above water level, but occasionally it may also nest colonially in trees, as at Lake Baringo in Kenya.

Black-headed Heron *Ardea melanocephala* KTU 96 cm

Immature

Adult

Similar to Grey Heron (p. 9) but with a *black head and hindneck* contrasting strongly with the white throat. The upperparts are dark grey, and the chest and belly are paler. Sexes are similar and immature is brownish grey with a darker grey heard. In flight the *underwing appears white*, contrasting with the black flight feathers, unlike the all-grey underwing. Mostly solitary, and usually feeds far from water in pastures. Nests communally, often in towns.

Purple Heron *Ardea purpurea* KTU 76 – 91 cm

Adult

Similar in appearance to Goliath Heron but *half the size*; also *much slimmer* with a long slender neck and a thin bill. Adult is grey and chestnut, with a rufous neck and a *black (not chestnut) crown*. The throat is white, and distinctive *black liners run from the gape to the nape and from the gape down the neck.* Immature is mottled brown and pale rufous, and black stripes on the head and neck are less distinct. Occurs in swamps and dense reedbeds in larger lakes, and is shy and solitary.

Common Squacco Heron *Ardeola ralloides* KTU 46 cm

This is a small, *short-legged* heron. Breeding birds are deep cinnamon-buff on the back,

Breeding adult

buff below, and develop long black-edged white plumes which reach as far as the tail. The bill is greenish yellow (black at the tip), the legs are yellowish and the eyes are yellow, but for a few days when breeding the bill turns blue and the legs turn red. Non-breeding and immature birds are pale grey-brown and strongly streaked, and have brown eyes. *On take-off, the wings are seen to be white, as are the rump and tail, and as such contrast strongly with the underparts.* Squaccos are mostly solitary and occur usually in dense vegetation in swamps, lakes and rivers.

Non-breeding adult

11

Cattle Egret *Bubulcus ibis* **KTU 51 cm**

Non-breeding adult

A small, short-ish-legged heron, entirely white, except during the breeding season when the crown, chest and mantle turn a rich buff colour. It has a *short yellow bill*, yellow eyes and *yellow-green legs*, all of which turn coral-red for a few days when breeding. Sexes are alike. Gregarious and tame, these birds occur in swamps, marshes, grasslands and pastures and often, but not always, in association with game and cattle.

Breeding adult

D. Richards

Great White Egret *Casmerodius albus* **KTU 89 – 92 cm**

Non-breeding adult

Largest of the white egrets and almost as large as Grey Heron (p. 9). It is all-white, slender-bodied and long-necked and has long, *all-black legs, a long, strong, yellow bill,* and a distinctive *thin black line extending from the gape to behind the eyes.* The similar Yellow-billed Egret (p. 13) is smaller and has a thin black line extending from the gape to immediately below the eyes. During breeding the bill turns black and long nuptial plumes grow down the back. Sexes are alike. Usually solitary, except when roosting or breeding, it occurs along the edges of swamps, lakes and rivers, in open water. Flies with its head and neck tucked tightly into its shoulders.

Breeding adult

D. Richards

Little Egret *Egretta garzetta* KTU 56 – 61 cm

An all-white medium-sized egret with a long neck, a *long black bill and black legs with distinctive bright yellow toes.* Breeding birds have long plumes from the head and nuptial plumes down the back. Sexes are alike, and immature is similar to non-breeding adult but has dull, not bright, yellow toes. Grey-coloured Little Egrets occur occasionally, most commonly along the coast from Mombasa southwards. Usually feeds alone or in loose groups in lakes, both fresh and soda, and along coastal waters. The Western Reef-Egret,

Adult

E. gularis, (not illustrated) has a white phase which may cause confusion but that bird has a larger, yellowish bill and pale legs.

Yellow-billed Egret (Intermediate Egret) *Egretta intermedia* KTU 66 cm

Non-breeding adult

Breeding adult

Similar to the Great White Egret but considerably smaller, shorter necked and with a *stumpy yellow bill.* The legs and toes are black but the upper leg is yellowish (often difficult to see). The eyes are yellow, and the *black line extending from the gape ends immediately below the eyes.* When breeding, the bill is orange, the eyes red and the area around the eyes green, and short plumes grow from the shoulders. Sexes are alike. Mostly solitary, it occurs in swamps, lakes and flooded areas.

13

Black-crowned Night Heron *Nycticorax nycticorax* KTU 61 cm

D. Richards

Adult

A medium-sized, short-legged heron with large red eyes. The black crown and back contrast strongly with the grey wings and white body. *Two distinctive, long, slender, white plumes* extend from the nape. Immature is pale brown with buffy spots on the back and wings; the underparts are paler with darker streaks. Usually found in small groups sitting in a characteristic *hunched position* in dense foliage along lakes and rivers. Although nocturnal, may be seen in late afternoon.

Hamerkop *Scopus umbretta* KTU 56 cm

D. Richards

Adult

An unmistakable, dull-brown, short-legged waterbird. The *hammer-shaped head*, with its large thick crest and large black bill, is distinctive. Sexes are alike and immature is very similar to adult but usually has a less pronounced head crest. Mostly feeds alone but sometimes feeds in loose groups, and occurs in almost any open shallow water. Builds a distinctive, domed nest, usually in the fork of a tree but occasionally on a rock; the small entrance often faces eastwards.

14

African Open-billed Stork *Anastomus lamelligerus* KTU **91 cm**

Adult

Immature

A medium-sized, *uniformly dark-plumaged* stork, with a long heavy bill which when closed has a characteristic *gap between the mandibles*. The sexes are alike, and immature is duller than adult and, depending on age, has a noticeably shorter bill with almost no gap. Highly gregarious, flocks often number in the thousands. Found in lakes, dams, floodplains and rice paddies. Uses its uniquely shaped bill to extract its main food of fresh-water snails from their shells.

Abdim's Stork *Ciconia abdimii* KTU **86 cm**

This small stork is black and white in colour. The head, back and wings are black with a purple-green gloss, and the lower back, upper tail and underparts are white. *The bare skin around the face is greenish and there is a red spot in front of the eyes. The bill is greenish with a red tip, and the legs are dull greenish with red joints.* Sexes are alike, but immature is browner and duller than adult. The similar Black Stork, *C. nigra*, (not illustrated) can be distinguished from Abdim's by its red bill and red legs. Tame and gregarious, Abdim's Storks frequently feed with White Storks (p. 16) in grasslands and pastures.

Adult

15

White Stork *Ciconia ciconia* KTU 102 cm

Adult

Unmistakable, this large white stork has black wings, a *bright red bill and red legs*. Sexes are alike, and immature is duller than adult, with a shorter, dull reddish bill and dull red legs. Gregarious birds, they are usually found feeding in grasslands and pastures, and are attracted to bush fires. Often seen soaring at great heights. In flight the tail appears all white which helps to distinguish it from the similar Yellow-billed Stork (p. 17) which shows an all-black tail in flight. Ringing recoveries show that most White Storks found in the region migrate from central Europe. Numbers appear to be much reduced compared with former years.

Saddle-billed Stork *Ephippiorhynchus senegalensis* KTU 168 cm

Male

Female

This striking unmistakable large, black and white stork has a *massive red sharp-pointed bill* with a black band around it and a distinctive yellow shield at its base. The black body often has a purple-green sheen. The legs are black with dull red joints and toes. There is also a bright red spot of naked skin on the chest. Sexes are similar but female has bright golden-yellow eyes and male has brown eyes and two small yellow wattles at the base of the bill (lacking in the female). Immature is duller and greyer than the adult, with a dull red and black bill which lacks a yellow shield. Occurs singly or in pairs in almost any aquatic habitat where there are fish.

16

Marabou Stork *Leptoptilos crumeniferus* KTU 150 cm

A large, ungainly-looking stork with a massive bill. The *bare pinkish skin of the head, neck and chest* are sparsely covered in down. A distensible, pink-coloured air sac hangs from the base of the neck. The wings and tail are glossy green-black and the bird's underparts are white. When breeding the bare skin intensifies in colour and there is a white border to the wing coverts. Sexes are alike, and immature is brownish with extensive woolly down on the head. Marabous often stand in a *characteristic hunched position* and, unlike other storks, fly with the head and neck tucked in. They occur almost everywhere, often alongside vultures at carcasses.

Adult

D. Richards

Yellow-billed Stork *Mycteria ibis* KTU 107 cm

D. Richards

Adult

A medium-sized, mostly white stork, immediately distinguished from White Stork by its *yellow bill* and its aquatic feeding habits. Adult is tinged with pink and has black wing tips, a black tail, *bare red skin on the forehead and face*, and a long yellow bill. When breeding, plumage is more diffused with pink and wing-covert tips are crimson. Sexes are alike, and immature is grey-brown with brown wing tips and tail, a pale yellow bill and brownish legs. Occurs in swamps, lakes and dams.

17

Hadeda Ibis *Bostrychia hagedash* KTU **76 cm**

Adult

Adult is a dull brown with a glossy green-bronze sheen on the shoulders and back, and a purple sheen on the wings. It has a long curved black bill (the upper mandible is mostly red) and a *distinctive white line on the cheeks.* Sexes are alike, and immature is duller than adult, with a shorter black bill. The well-known 'haa-de-daa' call is heard mostly at dawn and dusk, or when the birds are disturbed. Occurs in pairs or small groups, preferring damp areas, swamps and pastures.

Sacred Ibis *Threskiornis aethiopicus* KTU **90 cm**

Adult

Unmistakable, this bird is mostly white with a contrasting naked *black head and neck, and a long decurved black bill*. In breeding plumage it grows long, black, ornamental plumes over the tail and the bare skin along the base of the underwing becomes bright red (seen only when wing is lifted). Sexes are alike, and immature is similar to adult but has black and white mottled feathers over the head and neck. This ibis is gregarious and typically flies in formation, when the birds' black wing tips can be seen. Occurs in swamps, floodplains, pastures and along rivers and lake shores.

18

African Spoonbill *Platalea alba* KTU **90 cm**

Adult

D. Richards

An unmistakable, all-white bird with a *distinctive, flattened, spoon-shaped bill*, bare red skin on the forehead and face and red legs. The upper mandible is blue-grey edged with red (seen at close range) and the lower mandible is darker. Sexes are alike but immature is duller, with a horn-coloured bill and dark legs. Occurs singly or in groups in swamps, floodplains and lakes, both fresh and soda. Birds *fly in V-formation with the neck outstretched* and the silhouette of the bill obvious.

Lesser Flamingo *Phoeniconaias minor* KTU **100 cm**

Unmistakable, this bird is best distinguished from the Greater Flamingo (p. 20) by its smaller size and deeper pink plumage. The *dark red, black-tipped bill* also distinguishes it and is diagnostic. Sexes are alike, and immature is drab greyish white, with a grey-brown bill and legs. Highly gregarious birds, they occur almost exclusively on alkaline lakes. Lesser Flamingos are surface feeders, filtering their food from the top few centimetres of the water. Greater Flamingos, by contrast, filter their food from the bottom mud in shallow water.

Adult

Greater Flamingo *Phoenicopterus ruber* KTU 130 -142 cm

Adult

A *larger bird than the Lesser Flamingo* (p. 19) and paler in colour. The body is pinkish white and the upper and lower wing coverts (best seen in flight) are bright coral-red. The *bill is pink with a black tip*. The red-coloured wings with black tips – best seen in flight – are distinctive. Sexes are alike, and immature is greyish white with a pale-coloured bill, which helps distinguish it from immature Lesser Flamingo, which has a dark bill. Occurs in much smaller numbers than does the Lesser Flamingo, in alkaline lakes, coastal areas and occasionally in fresh-water lakes. Feeds by filtering food from the bottom mud of shallow waters.

D. Richards

White-faced Whistling-Duck *Dendrocygna viduata* KTU 48 cm

'*dult*

A distinctive duck with a *characteristic upright stance.* The body plumage is rich brown and black with barred flanks, and the *face, throat and forehead are white* but are often stained through feeding in muddy water. The bill is black with a blue bar at the tip and the legs and feet are blue. Sexes are alike and immature is similar to adult but has a greyish face, throat and forehead. Gregarious, and at times very common. Occurs in large numbers in swamps, lakes, floodplains, dams and flooded margins of rivers, where its clear whistling call is a feature.

. Richards

Egyptian Goose *Alopochen aegyptiacus* **KTU 62 cm**

Adults

A large brown waterbird with pink legs and a pink bill. The *conspicuous rufous patch around the eyes and the dark patch in the centre of the belly* are diagnostic. The white patch in the wing is particularly noticeable in flight. Sexes are similar and immature resembles adult but is duller and lacks the dark chest patch and rufous eye-patch. At times can be very noisy. Common, and usually found in pairs in almost any water habitat. When moulting they gather in large numbers.

Northern Pintail *Anas acuta* **KTU m = 66 cm; f = 56 cm**

Male

Female

A *slender-bodied, long-necked and long-tailed* migrant duck. Male in nuptial plumage is unmistakable with its chocolate-brown head, *distinctive white stripe from behind the eyes to the foreneck*, its white breast, grey upperparts and its *long pointed tail*. Female, and male in eclipse plumage are mottled brown with a shorter tail. In flight the pale underparts and pointed wings and tail are distinctive. Occurs in freshwater lakes in the highlands.

21

Cape Teal *Anas capensis* **KT 35 cm**

R.S. Daniell

Adults

A small, pale, speckled duck with a *bright pink slightly upturned bill*. The wing is darker and in flight shows a blue speculum. Sexes are alike and immature is similar to adult. A *characteristic duck of the alkaline lakes*, and usually found in pairs or small groups, although occasionally large flocks do occur in the Rift Valley lakes. Feeds mostly by sieving the top surface of the water (much like a Lesser Flamingo) for aquatic food items.

Northern Shoveler *Anas clypeata* **KTU 51 cm**

D. Richards

Breeding male

P. Davey

Female

A large migrant duck with a *distinctive large spatulate bill*. Male in breeding plumage is unmistakable with a dark green head, a white neck and breast, bright chestnut on the belly and flanks, and bright yellow eyes. Female and non-breeding male are brown. Occurs singly or in small groups, in both fresh-water and in alkaline lakes. Found mostly in the west and central highlands of Kenya. Occasionally, tens of thousands occur on Lake Turkana, Old Bolosat and Nakuru, where it is the commonest wintering duck, becoming much less common further south.

22

Red-billed Teal *Anas erythrorhyncha* KTU 38 cm

Adult

D. Richards

A medium-sized, red-billed, buffy duck mottled with brown spots. May be confused with Cape Teal (both having a red bill) but *distinguished from that bird by its distinctive dark cap which contrasts with paler cheeks, and also by its larger size.* The wing is dark with a pink speculum, and in flight it shows pale secondaries. Sexes are alike, and immature is similar to adult but is generally duller. Occurs in small groups on lakes, dams and floodplains.

Hottentot Teal *Anas hottentota* KTU 28 cm

Adult

D. Richards

Africa's *smallest duck with a blue bill and a distinctive dark cap.* The body is brown and the wing is darker and in flight shows a green speculum edged with white and a distinctive white trailing edge. Sexes are similar, and immature is duller than adult with a brown-blue bill. Distinguished from Red-billed Teal by its smaller size and its blue bill. Prefers shallow water, swamps, marshes, dams and ponds, and is usually found in pairs or in small groups.

23

Gargany *Anas querquedula* KTU 38 cm

D. Richards

Breeding male

D. Richards

Female

A small migrant duck with white streaks above and below the eyes. Male in breeding plumage is distinctive, with a *broad white stripe from the eyes to the nape,* and grey flanks. Female resembles non-breeding male: buffy brown with a darker crown and pale eyestrip. Occurs singly or in small groups, usually in shallow waters.

Yellow-billed Duck *Anas undulata* KTU 54 cm

D. Richards

Adult

A distinctive duck with a *bright yellow bill* which has a black patch on the upper mandible and a black tip. The head is grey, finely streaked, and the body is grey-brown with pale-edged feathers. The green speculum is seen in flight. Sexes are similar and immature is duller than adult. A *characteristic duck,* usually found in pairs or in small groups *on fresh-water* lakes, swamps and dams, especially in the highlands above 1 600 m where it is the commonest resident duck.

Southern Pochard *Netta erythrophthalma* **KTU 46 cm**

Female (left) *and male* (right)

A brown duck with a blue-grey bill. The male has *distinctive red eyes* and the head is darker than the body. The *female* is duller with a white throat, dark eyes, and a *distinctive pale-whitish, crescent-shaped mark on the side of the head*. In flight both sexes show a distinctive *white bar in the wing*. Immature resembles female but is paler. Prefers deep, mainly fresh-water lakes. Male Maccoa Duck, *Oxyura maccoa*, (not illustrated) is distinguished by its chestnut body and bright blue bill.

Secretary Bird *Sagittarius serpentarius* **KTU 140 cm**

Adult

An unmistakable, *large, slim, grey bird with long legs, black wings,* a long graduated tail, and an orange-red face. The *conspicuous, long, loose crest of black feathers on the nape* is often raised when the bird is excited. In flight, the legs extend well beyond the tail. Sexes are similar, and immature is brownish grey with a shorter tail and a yellow face. Usually seen walking in grasslands and open areas, singly or in pairs. Perches and nests in small trees or tall bushes.

25

African White-backed Vulture *Gyps africanus* KTU **81 cm**

A large, uniform brown vulture with a dark head and neck and a white ruff at the base of the neck. The *eyes are dark* and the *bill is black*. The white back and rump are seen only in flight or when the wings are held open. The *white forewing* (seen in flight) *is distinctive*. Sexes are alike but immature is a darker uniform

Adults

Adult in flight

brown without white on the back or rump. Roosts and nests in trees, often near water. The commonest vulture of game country.

Rüppell's Griffon Vulture *Gyps rueppellii* KTU **86 cm**

Adult

Adult in flight

A large brown vulture, distinguished from African White-backed Vulture by the *creamy white edging to the feathers, which imparts a scaly appearance*. The head and neck are grey, the cere and face blue-grey, the bill horn-coloured tinged with pink, and the eyes are bright orange-yellow. The blue-grey bare patches on either side of the crop are distinctive as are the *three narrow whitish bars seen on the underwing* in flight. Sexes are similar, and immature is paler than adult and has a dark bill. Immature is distinguished from immature African White-backed Vulture by its paler colour, longer neck and larger bill. Habitually perches and nests on cliffs, although will perch in trees. Occurs in game country and open areas, especially near cliffs.

Lappet-faced Vulture *Torgos tracheliotus* **KTU 101 cm**

Adult

Adult in flight

The largest African vulture. The *crimson-coloured bare skin on the head and neck and the massive greenish-brown bill* are diagnostic. The feathers on the flank are white and contrast with the dark body. Sexes are similar, and immature resembles adult but has pale pink bare skin on the head and neck, and dark, not white, flanks. When seen from below *in flight* the long, broad wings with a *white streak near the forewing and the white flanks* are distinctive.

African Harrier Hawk (Gymnogene) *Polyboroides typus* **KTU 61 – 68 cm**

Adult

Adult in flight

A distinctive *long-legged and long-tailed grey hawk*. The head *is small* and there is *yellow bare skin on the face*, which during breeding or when the bird is excited turns bright red. The feathers on the back of the head are long and sometimes raised to form a broad crest. The legs are yellow. Sexes are similar but female is larger than male. Immature is brown with a characteristic small head. *In flight the broad grey wings with contrasting black primaries and secondaries*, and the *long black tail with its white bar* are distinctive. Usually occurs in forests, woodlands and in savannah country with large trees. Searches for prey by clinging to tree trunks or hanging upside-down from weavers' nests, usually with its wings flapping.

27

Brown Snake-Eagle *Circaetus cinereus* **KTU 66 – 68 cm**

Adult in flight

This all-brown eagle has a distinctive, almost *owl-like head, large yellow eyes and bare unfeathered legs.* Sexes are alike but female is a little larger. Immature is paler than adult with a scaly appearance and the bare legs. *In flight the dark body and underwings contrast with the paler flight feathers and three pale bands in the tail.* Usually seen perched in a characteristic erect stance, high up in a tree in savannah country.

Adult

Black-chested Snake-Eagle *Circaetus pectoralis* **KTU 68 – 71 cm**

Adult in flight

Like the Brown Snake-Eagle with its characteristic *owl-like head, yellow eyes*, dark underparts, bare legs and distinctive erect stance, but differs in having *white underparts.* Sexes are similar. *In flight the white belly and wings and barred tail* are conspicuous. Immature is pale brown with no white on the underparts and is thus difficult to separate from Brown Snake-Eagle. Usually seen perched high in a tree or soaring. Frequently hovers (only eagle to do so regularly) over savannahs and light woodland.

Adult

28

Bateleur *Terathopius ecaudatus* **KTU 55 – 70 cm**

D. Richards

Adult male

D. Richards

Immature

A distinctive, mainly black eagle with a chestnut back, a very short tail, a red face and red legs. Unmistakable in flight when the black body contrasts with the long white wings, and the red legs protrude beyond the tail. Sexes are similar but in flight male shows a broad black trailing edge to the wing compared to the thin black trailing edge of the female's wing. Immature is all brown with a short tail (although longer than adult's), a distinctive large head and greenish-blue cere which distinguishes it from other generally brown eagles. Mostly seen in flight over savannah country below 3 000 m.

D. Richards

Male in flight

D. Richards

Female in flight

Shikra (Little Banded Goshawk) *Accipiter badius* KTU 28 – 33 cm

A small, swift-flying hawk. The head, back and wings are uniform grey and the underparts are finely barred up to the chin and appear pinkish. The *red eyes and yellow legs* are distinctive. Sexes are similar but female is larger than the male, has a darker back and is more heavily barred below. Immature is brownish with heavy blotching on the underparts and has yellow-orange eyes and yellow-orange legs. In flight the short wings, long tail and *all-grey upperparts are diagnostic*; tail shows bars when seen from below. Occurs in savannah, woodland and acacia country, tending to avoid dense forest and very dry regions.

Adult

D. Richards

African Goshawk *Accipiter tachiro* KTU 36 – 43 cm

SIL / P. Pickford

Adult

Immature

D. Richards

Similar to the Shikra but larger, darker grey on the upperparts and with a barred upper tail. The underparts are barred brown-rufous and the *eyes, cere and legs are yellow*. Female is larger and browner than male. Immature is dark brown above and pale below with heavy dark blotches. Commonly occurring in highland forests and usually seen flying over the forest with a characteristic, fast wing-beat followed by a short glide, while uttering a 'krik, krik' call.

30

Steppe Eagle *Aquila nipalensis* **KTU 75 cm**

Adult

A large, stout-looking eagle, usually uniform dark brown although some birds have a pale patch on the crown or nape. The bill is large, the nostrils oval and the *yellow gape extends to behind the eyes*. The legs are heavy and feathered. Immature is paler with pale bars in the wing. In flight the wings show a distinctive white trailing edge. *Habitually perches on the ground or on low rocks.* Occurs in small groups or in flocks, usually in open country. A migrant, common in March and April.

Tawny Eagle *Aquila rapax* **KTU 66 – 72 cm**

Adult (pale phase)

Adult (dark phase)

A mostly uniform brown eagle, although the plumage can vary considerably from dark brown to almost white. Distinguished from similar Steppe Eagle only at close range when *bill is seen to be smaller and yellow gape is seen to extend as far as the centre of the eye*, not beyond it. Sexes are similar but female is larger. Can be told from Brown Snake-Eagle (p. 28) by its smaller head, darker eyes and feathered legs. Immature is paler than adult, and shows pale bars in the wing although these are not as distinct as in immature Steppe Eagle. Oc singly or in pairs and is usual perched in a tree or soaring open country. Tawny Eagle known for raiding weaver c

Verreaux's Eagle *Aquila verreauxii* KTU 76 – 81 cm

Adult

A large black eagle that shows a distinctive white V-mark on the back. The legs and feet are yellow. *In flight the wing shape* (narrow at the base) and *white patches in the wing are unique.* Sexes are similar but female is larger. Immature is mottled brown with rufous on the crown and nape, and in flight shows distinctive wing shape of adult. Usually found where there are cliffs and kopjes. Preys mainly on Rock Hyrax but also takes other mammals, such as hares. A very localised species; the best-known pair in the region can be seen at Lake Baringo, Kenya, on nearby cliffs where they also breed.

Adult in flight

Augur Buzzard *Buteo augur* KTU 50 – 57 cm

Adult

The head, sides of the neck and back of this bird are black, the underparts are white and it has a *distinctive rufous tail.* The eyes are dark and cere and gape are yellow. Melanistic birds – all black apart from barred grey-black wing feathers and a rufous tail – are not uncommon. Sexes are similar but female is larger. Immature is brownish white streaked underparts and a pale rufous tail. Occurs mostly in the highlands but also in low country where there are isolated hills.

Photo credits: R.S. Daniell; D. Richards

African Hawk-Eagle *Hieraaetus spilogaster* KTU 61 – 71 cm

Adult

D. Richards

Black above and white below with black streaks on the throat and breast. The cere, eye and feet are yellow. Sexes are similar but female is larger and more heavily streaked below. Immature has brown upperparts and buffy underparts. *In flight, the dark forewing and black band at end of tail contrast with the white underparts.* Often confused with Augur Buzzard, but larger size, streaked front and feathered legs distinguish it. Found in savannah woodland, forests and thornbush country.

Long-crested Eagle *Lophaetus occipitalis* KTU 51 – 56 cm

This small eagle with its distinctive long loose crest is unmistakable. The body is dark brown, appearing black, and contrasts with the mainly *white, feathered legs.* Sexes are similar but female is larger than male, and male has a longer head crest then female. Immature has a shorter crest and grey (not yellow) eyes, but is otherwise similar to adult. *In flight, the white patches in the wing, the white legs and the black and white barred* tail distinguish this eagle. Commonly seen perched

Adult

D. Richards

Adult in flight

D. Richards

along highways on telephone and power poles. It prefers well-wooded country in high-rainfall areas up to 2 000-m altitudes but also adapts well to cultivated land.

Gabar Goshawk *Micronisus gabar* KTU 30 – 34 cm

Adult (grey form)

This goshawk occurs in two distinct colour phases: a grey form – the more common form – and a melanistic form. The grey form has a grey *Adult (melanistic form)* head, back, throat and breast, a *white rump*, finely barred underparts, a barred tail, and *red eyes, cere and legs*. Female is larger and more heavily barred than male. The melanistic form is all black (lacks the white rump) with a barred tail and red eyes, a red cere and red legs. Immature is brown, boldly blotched, with a white rump, yellow eyes and a pale orange cere and legs. Usually found in woodland and in thornbush country.

Dark Chanting-Goshawk *Melierax metabates* KTU 49 cm

Adult

An all-dark-grey hawk with a finely barred rump, red-brown eyes and a *red cere and legs*. Sexes are similar but female is slightly larger. Immature is brown above and streaked below, with yellow eyes, a grey cere and greyish-yellow legs. Usually seen sitting in an upright stance on a low tree or bush. Occurs in open country and light woodland, west of the Rift Valley. Overlaps with Eastern Chanting-Goshawk near Baringo and Kedong Valley (Kenya) and in the southern part of the Serengeti.

Eastern Chanting-Goshawk *Melierax poliopterus* **KTU 51 cm**

Much paler than Dark Chanting-Goshawk and larger than the similar-looking Gabar Goshawk. The upperparts, head and neck are pale grey with a distinctive white rump, the breast and belly are finely barred grey, the eyes are red, *the cere is yellow and the legs are orange*. Sexes are similar but female is larger than male. Immature is pale brown with a white rump, whitish eyes, a grey cere and pale yellow legs. Displays similar habitats to Dark Chanting-Goshawk, but occurs east of the Rift Valley in more arid country. Very common in these

Adult

parts, especially in the Samburu District, Kenya. (See Dark Chanting-Goshawk, opposite below, for areas of overlap).

Martial Eagle *Polemaetus bellicosus* **KTU 76 – 86 cm**

Adult

Adult in flight

Africa's largest eagle. A large, powerful bird with a small crest on the nape. The back, throat and upper breast are brownish grey, and the *underparts are white with small dark spots*. Female is larger and more heavily spotted than male. Immature has pale brown upperparts, face and throat, and white underparts. Differs from Black-chested Snake-Eagle (p. 28) by its larger size, spotted underparts, feathered legs and dark, not pale, underwing (seen in flight). Occurs in acacia savannahs and thornbush.

35

African Crowned Eagle *Stephanoaetus coronatus* KTU 80 – 92 cm

Male

Adult (showing wing pattern)

A large, powerful eagle with short broad wings, a long tail and a *conspicuous head crest*. The upperparts are dark, while the breast and belly are rufous with dark bars or blotching. The eyes are pale yellow, and the cere and legs are yellow. Sexes are similar but female is larger than male.

Immature has pale grey-brown upperparts, a white head (distinguishing it from immature Martial Eagle, p. 35, which has a brown head), and is white below with some spotting on the thighs and legs. Occurs in highland forests, and is most often seen flying over the forests in display flight, or perched in the forest over a game trail.

African Fish Eagle *Haliaeetus vocifer* KTU 63 – 76 cm

Adult

A distinctive eagle, easily recognised by the *white head, chest, back and tail* and the contrasting *chestnut belly and shoulders* and black wings. Sexes are similar but female is larger. Immature is duller than adult, and heavily streaked which could cause confusion with migrating ospreys. The loud yelping call of both sexes, often given in duet, is one of Africa's most distinctive sounds. Occurs in association with almost any water habitat. Feeds almost entirely on fish.

36

Black Kite *Milvus migrans* **KTU 53 – 58 cm**

D. Richards

Adult in flight

P.J. Frere

An all-brown bird with a conspicuous *yellow bill*, brown eyes and a distinctive *forked tail*. Sexes are similar and immature resembles adult but shows streaking on the chest and belly, a

Adult

black bill, and a less distinctly forked tail. A Eurasian race of this species, which visits East Africa from September to April, differs in being slightly darker and in having a smaller, paler head finely streaked black, a black bill, pale eyes and a less distinctly forked tail. Mainly a scavenger, found around cities and towns and around fishing villages on shores of Lake Victoria. Flies earlier than other raptors, often seen soon after sunrise quartering roads for road kills.

Black-shouldered Kite *Elanus caeruleus* **KTU 33 cm**

This small greyish raptor is *often seen hovering* above open land or conspicuously perched on top of a tree or telephone pole, flicking its tail up and down. The head, underparts and tail are white, the back is grey, and there is a *distinctive black patch on the shoulder*. The feet and the cere are bright yellow and the *eyes are deep red.* Sexes are similar, and immature is darker than adult with white tips to the mantle and wing feathers, and yellow eyes. Most often found hunting over open cultivated land, grassland or along roadside verges where it preys on rodents.

Adult

Lesser Kestrel *Falco naumanni* **KTU 30 cm**

Male

A migrant bird, small and gregarious, and at times very common. Male differs from other kestrels by its *smaller size, uniform chestnut back* and generally paler appearance. Female and immature are mainly buffy brown with darker streaks and spots, and have a barred brown tail. At close range the distinctive white claws can be seen. Usually occurs in loose flocks over grassland and open cultivated country. Most commonly enters the region during October/November on its passage southwards and again in March/April on its passage north.

Female

Greater Kestrel (White-eyed Kestrel) *Falco rupicoloides* **KTU 36 cm**

Similar to female Kestrel but *larger*, more heavily barred, and with a pale grey rump, a pale, grey-black barred tail and distinctive *pale creamy eyes*. The cere and the feet are yellow. Sexes are similar, and immature resembles adult but has dark eyes. Occurs sparsely in open acacia and semi-desert areas. Locally common below 1 800 m. Hunts mostly from a perch, rarely hovering (unlike other kestrels). Feeds mainly on small mammals and lizards. Breeds in the abandoned nests of Cape Rooks (p. 91), unlike other kestrels – which are cliff-nesters.

Adult

Common Kestrel *Falco tinnunculus* KTU 33 – 36 cm

Female

Male

Similar in appearance to the Lesser Kestrel but slightly larger. Male has *distinctive black spotting on the back*. Two races occur in East Africa, one a migrant from Eurasia. The local race is usually darker and the female has a grey-barred tail (migrant female has a brown-barred tail). The local kestrels occur in pairs, usually near rocks and cliffs; migrants generally occur in small flocks in open country. Both races hunt by hovering before dropping on their prey.

Pygmy Falcon *Polihierax semitorquatus* KTU 18 – 20 cm

Male

A *tiny, stocky* shrike-sized falcon, with a distinctive *red cere and coral-red legs*. The upperparts are grey with a white collar, and the face, underparts and uppertail coverts are white. In flight the wings and tail are seen to be black with white spots. *Female* is similar to male but shows a *chestnut mantle*, and immature resembles adults but is duller. Occurs in semi-desert, thornbush country and savannahs, where it can be seen perched conspicuously on bushes and trees. Often found near Buffalo Weavers' nests, in which it breeds.

Female

Red-necked Spurfowl *Francolinus afer* KTU 33 – 36 cm

Adult

Varies in colour from grey to brown with the underparts streaked chestnut or black and white. The *red throat, red bill and red legs* are distinctive. Sexes are alike, but female is smaller than male. Immature is similar to adult but duller. Occurs in light woodland and savannah country with thickets, usually in pairs or in small family parties. The Grey-breasted Spurfowl, *F. rufopictus*, (not illustrated) is similar but can be distinguished by its bright orange throat.

Coqui Francolin *Francolinus coqui* KTU 20 – 25 cm

Male (left) *and female* (right)

The smallest francolin, with an *orange-yellow head and neck* and paler throat. The underparts are barred black and white, and the feet are yellow. Female is similar to male but has a black line below the eyes which extends to below the white throat. Immature is paler than adult. Usually occurs in pairs or in small coveys in grasslands and savannah woodlands. The call, a distinctive 'co-qe, co-qe' which gets gradually louder, is a feature of the East African grasslands.

40

Yellow-necked Spurfowl *Francolinus leucoscepus* KTU 33 – 36 cm

The *bright yellow throat and red bare skin around the eyes* of this spurfowl are distinctive. The upperparts are greyish brown streaked whitish, and the underparts are paler with buffy streaks. In flight, the pale wing patches are very conspicuous (helping to distinguish it from the Red-necked Spurfowl). Sexes are alike, and immature is similar to adult but has less pronounced streaking. Most often seen sitting on a low prominent perch – a low horizontal branch or a termite mound – in a distinctive upright stance.

Adult

D. Richards

A common bird, occurring in dry bush country and savannahs, and usually found in pairs or in small family parties.

Crested Francolin *Francolinus sephaena* KTU 22 – 28 cm

Adults

D. Richards

A *mainly brown francolin* with a distinctive white eye-stripe, white streaking on the upperparts, and buffy underparts with darker triangular spots on the sides of the neck. The dark crest on the head is only seen when the bird is excited. The legs are red, and the tail is typically held cocked at a 45 degree angle. In flight, the black tail is conspicuous. Sexes are similar, and immature resembles adult but is duller. Found in small parties in dry bush country, often near water courses.

Vulturine Guineafowl *Acryllium vulturinum* KT 58 – 61 cm

D. Richards

Adult

A large, distinctive-looking guineafowl with long legs and with long, pointed tail feathers. The *small, grey-coloured bare head with a tuft of velvety brown feathers on the nape is characteristic*. The feathers of the neck and chest are long and pointed with white stripes and cobalt-blue edges, and the breast and sides of the chest are bright cobalt-blue. The back, belly and wings are black with small white spots. Sexes are alike but female is slightly smaller than the male. Immature is duller than adult. Highly gregarious, occurring in large flocks in dry desert and thornbush country. Usually seen at dawn and dusk, often when approaching water.

Helmeted Guineafowl *Numida meleagris* KTU 51 – 56 cm

D. Richards

Adult

A familiar, easily recognised bird, overall greyish black in colour with small white spots. The *bright blue face and neck, the horn-coloured bony crest* (which varies in shape and length throughout the region), *and the red-tipped blue wattles* are distinctive. Sexes are similar, and immature is drabber than adult with a smaller and duller crest and smaller, duller wattles. Found in savannah, thornbush, and cultivated areas, usually in flocks, and is most active at dawn and dusk.

42

Grey Crowned Crane *Balearica regulorum* **KTU 102 cm**

Adults

A distinctive, long-legged bird with a *conspicuous golden-yellow tuft on the crown,* a bold *white patch on the cheeks, a black forehead and red wattles.* The upperparts are slate grey, the underparts are paler, and the wing is blackish with a distinctive white-tinged chestnut patch. Sexes are alike, and immature is brownish with a smaller head tuft. Usually found in pairs, but occasionally in large flocks outside of the breeding season, around swamps, lakes and in grasslands.

Common Moorhen *Gallinula chloropus* **KTU 33 cm**

Adult

An all-black aquatic bird with a *bright red frontal shield,* red eyes and a *yellow-tipped red bill.* It has *conspicuous white marks along the flanks, and white feathers under the tail* which is usually held high. The legs are green with a red band above the joint. Moves with a very jerky motion when swimming and walking, and continually flicks its tail. Sexes are alike, and immature is duller with a greenish-brown bill and legs. Found in fresh-water lakes, swamps, dams and ponds.

R.S. Daniell

D. Richards

43

Black Crake *Amaurornis flavirostris* KTU 20 cm

Adults

A small all-black bird with a *distinctive bright chrome-yellow bill, deep red eyes and bright red legs*, especially noticeable when breeding. Sexes are alike, and immature is greyish brown with a green-brown bill and brown legs. Usually seen in pairs or small loose groups feeding along the water's edge or on waterlilies, and often on the backs of hippos. Occurs in almost any fresh-water habitat as long as there is dense vegetation in which to take cover.

Red-knobbed Coot *Fulica cristata* KTU 41 cm

Adult

Larger than the Black Crake and also distinguished by its *characteristic white forehead and white bill*. The eyes are deep red and there are red knobs above the forehead, often only visible during breeding. The legs and feet are green. Sexes are identical. Immature is ashy brown overall, and is distinguished from immature Moorhen (p. 43) by its lack of white undertail coverts. Found in large open waters, singly or in large flocks. Dives for food but may also feed along the shoreline.

44

Black-bellied Bustard *Eupodotis melanogaster* **KTU 61 cm**

A *long-necked, long-legged, slender* bustard. The upperparts are brown with blackish vermiculations, the *rump is brown*, and the *tail is brown with indistinct bars.* There is a distinctive thin black line behind each eye and, in the male, a black line extending from the grey throat down the neck to merge with the black belly. Female is paler, with a whitish belly and does not show black line down the neck. Hartlaub's Bustard, *E. hartlaubii*, (not illustrated) is very similar but differs by being stockier, greyer in appearance and with a black rump and tail. Female Hartlaub's is very similar to female Black-bellied but has a whitish line down the neck merging with a pale belly. Black-bellied Bustards occur singly, or occasionally in pairs, in grasslands.

Male

Female

Buff-crested Bustard *Eupodotis ruficrista* **KTU 53 cm**

Male

This bustard also has a black belly but is *smaller and stockier* than the Black-bellied Bustard, and has sandy-coloured

Female

upperparts, wings edged with white, and the *top of the head grey with pinkish-buffy face and crest. The throat is black and a black line edged with white extends down the neck to merge with the belly.* Female is paler, with the top of the head grey speckled with white, a white throat and a white-speckled foreneck, becoming completely white on the lower chest. Immature is similar to female but lacks white spots down the neck. Displaying males fly upwards vertically, tip over, and drop to the ground, opening their wings just before landing. Occurs singly in dry thornbush country.

45

White-bellied Bustard *Eupodotis senegalensis* **KTU 61 cm**

Male

Female

Usually the commonest bustard seen on safari. Male is distinctive with a *blue-grey neck*, white face and a blackish-brown crown. The upperparts are brown with fine, dark brown vermiculations. Female and immature are duller than male, with a brown crown and hindneck and a brownish-grey foreneck. Occurs in pairs or in small family groups in grasslands and savannahs. The call is a rhythmical croaking, uttered repeatedly at dawn and dusk. Male in display approaches female with neck stretched forwards and throat puffed out, all the feathers on the throat and neck being erect at this time.

Kori Bustard *Ardeotis kori* **KTU 76 – 101 cm**

Male displaying   *Adult*

The largest bustard, with a *distinctive dark head crest and a finely barred grey neck*. The upperparts are brown and the underparts are whitish. Female is similar to male but 20 per cent smaller, and immature resembles adult but has duller plumage. Male performs a distinctive courtship display, with crest raised, throat puffed out, wings drooped and tail cocked to meet head, revealing white undertail coverts. Usually seen striding across grasslands and open semi-desert country.

African Jacana *Actophilornis africanus* KTU 23 – 28 cm

Adult

A bright *chestnut bird with long legs and long toes.* The head is distinctive with a black crown and hindneck, a white face and foreneck with a golden-yellow band at the base, and a blue bill and frontal shield. Sexes are similar but female is larger than male. Immature is browner than adult and has a grey bill and frontal shield. Occurs in pairs and small family parties on almost any fresh water with floating vegetation. Females are polyandrous, and the males incubate and rear the young.

Common Ringed Plover *Charadrius hiaticula* KTU 19 cm

Adult

A small sturdy plover with distinctive *black and white forehead bands and a black band through the eyes.* The throat and underparts are white separated by a black band, the upperparts and crown are brown, the bill is orange with a black tip, and the legs are orange-yellow. A *conspicuous white wing bar* is visible in flight. Sexes are similar, and immature is paler with no black bands on the forehead, a brown band through the eye, and with a brown, often incomplete chest band.

47

Kittlitz's Plover *Charadrius pecuarius* KTU 14 cm

Adult

This small, neat and tame plover is brown above and on top of the head, and has a white throat and forehead. A white line from behind the eye extends around the back of the neck to form a distinctive collar, and a black band on the forehead extends through and behind the eye and around the neck. The chest and upper belly are rich rufous (especially in breeding male) and the remaining underparts are white. Sexes are similar, and immature is duller than adult, and has a brownish-buff chest; lacks black band on forehead and through the eyes. Most commonly occurs on salt flats surrounding soda lakes.

Three-banded Plover *Charadrius tricollaris* KTU 18 cm

Adult

A little larger than Kittlitz's Plover and with *two distinctive black bands, separated by a white band, across the chest*. The forehead is white, the throat grey, and a white line extends from the forehead to behind the nape. The *large red ring around each eye and the black-tipped red bill* are conspicuous. Separated from Ringed Plover (p. 47) by its smaller size and by its distinctive chest bands. Sexes are alike, and immature is mainly brownish, with brown, often incomplete chest bands. Occurs most often in pairs along muddy edges of rivers, lakes and swamps. Has a distinctive habit of *bobbing its head and tail.*

Blacksmith Plover (Blacksmith Lapwing) *Vanellus armatus* **KT 30 cm**

This large conspicuous *black, white and greyish plover* has deep-red eyes, a black bill and black legs. Sexes are similar, and immature resembles adult but is browner and has a buff forehead. Occurs singly or in pairs on dry ground alongside lakes, rivers and swamps. May occur in large flocks outside of the breeding season. Gives a very distinctive metallic 'tink tink' call when alarmed. Breeding birds are very aggressive towards intruders, dive-bombing anyone that threatens the nest. The Long-toed Plover, *V. crassirostris*, (not illustrated) also has a white crown, neck and throat but occurs in aquatic habitats, not on dry ground.

Adult

D. Richards

Crowned Plover (Crowned Lapwing) *Vanellus coronatus* **KTU 28 cm**

A common, largely uniform plover with a *distinctive black cap ringed with white*, and a black forehead extending to behind the eyes. The throat and chest are brown, edged on the lower breast with a thin black line, and the belly is white. The black-tipped red bill, bright red legs and bright yellow eyes are also distinctive. Sexes are similar, and immature resembles adult but is duller. Occurs in pairs in short grass plains and semi-desert country, showing no affinity for water. A gregarious bird, except when breeding, and also very noisy.

Adult

D. Richards

49

African Wattled Plover (African Wattled Lapwing) *Vanellus senegallus* KTU 33 cm

Adult

D. Richards

This large grey-brown plover has distinctive *yellow wattles hanging from in front of the eyes*, the smaller red wattles above the yellow ones. The forehead is white, the centre of the chin is black, and the face and neck are streaked with black. A thin black line separates the brown chest and upper belly. The bill is yellow with a black tip, and the *legs and feet are yellow*. Sexes are alike, and immature is similar to adult but is duller overall. Has a distinctive upright stance (when wing spurs can often be seen). Occurs in pairs in damp areas around lakes, streams, marshes and pools; also in short open grasslands.

Spur-wing Plover (Spur-wing Lapwing) *Vanellus spinosus* KTU 27 cm

Adult

D. Richards

A mainly black, brown and white plover. Differs from Blacksmith Plover (p. 49) by its slightly crested *black crown and black throat which contrast with the white cheeks and neck*. The back and wings are pale brown, the bill is black, as are the legs and feet, and it has dull red eyes. Sexes are alike, and immature resembles adult but is duller. Hybrids of this species and the Blacksmith Plover occur from time to time, causing identification problems. Usually occurs in pairs in short grass alongside rivers, marshes, and soda and fresh-water lakes.

Common Sandpiper *Actitis hypoleucos* KTU 20 cm

Adult

D. Richards

A small wader with a short, sharp bill and short greenish legs. The dark grey-brown upperparts contrast with the white underparts, and the white on the breast curves over the shoulder. Has a characteristic horizontal stance, and often bobs its head and tail. When disturbed it flies low over the water with flickering wings and a distinctive 'twee, tweee, wee' call. Shows a white wing bar in flight. A visitor to East Africa, and usually solitary along rivers, streams and lake shores.

Whimbrel *Numenius phaeopus* KTU 41 cm

Adult

D. Richards

A large, brown, long-legged wading bird with a distinctive, *long, curved bill*. At close range two dark and one pale stripe can be seen on the head. In flight it gives a distinctive trill and the *white rump and lower back* are conspicuous. Sexes are alike but female is slightly larger. A visitor to East Africa from Eurasia, it occurs singly or in small groups along the coast, especially in creeks and lagoons. Small numbers also regularly occur inland, mainly at the Rift Valley soda lakes.

Wood Sandpiper *Tringa glareola* KTU 20 cm

Adult

The most common wader in the region, with a characteristic *spotted appearance*, and a distinctive *pale eyebrow*. The upperparts are dark brown and the underparts are paler, though not white as in the Common Sandpiper (p. 51). Also has a more upright stance than Common Sandpiper and head-bobbing is not as pronounced. In flight it shows a white rump, and its legs protrude beyond the tail. Sexes are alike. A visitor from Eurasia, found mostly inland at almost any fresh water.

Common Greenshank *Tringa nebularia* KTU 32 cm

Adult

A common, pale grey, long-legged wader with a *long, pointed, slightly upturned bill*. The underparts are white and the legs are grey-green. In flight the *white rump and back* are conspicuous. Utters a very distinctive 'chew, chew' call, and when feeding has a habit of dashing about in shallow water. Sexes are alike, and immature resembles adult. A visitor from Eurasia, it occurs mostly singly or in small loose parties around almost any water – coastal and inland.

52

Little Stint *Calidris minuta* **KTU 13 cm**

Adult

A very *common, small, compact-looking* wader with a *short, straight, black bill*. The upperparts are brown with a mottled appearance (feathers have dark centres) and the underparts are pale, but in April the breast is often a rich brown. Sexes are alike. Always busy, feeding or running along the shoreline. A visitor from Eurasia, occurring singly or in small groups, but sometimes seen in large flocks when migrating. Found along coastal and inland waters.

Ruff *Philomachus pugnax* **KTU 24 – 30 cm**

Non-breeding adult

A common wader, stocky-bodied and with a *short, straight, black bill and orange legs*. The upperparts are

Transitional adult

mottled brown (pale edges to the dark feathers) and the underparts are paler. Sexes are alike but male is larger than female; males with completely white heads occasionally occur. A visitor to East Africa from Eurasia, it occurs in loose groups in flooded grasslands and coastal and inland waters. Often confused with the Common Redshank, *Tringa tetanus*, (not illustrated), but that bird is mainly grey with a long, straight bill, bright red legs, and is usually solitary. Also, Redshank shows a conspicuous white rump and a white hind-wing in flight, which are lacking in the Ruff.

53

Black-winged Stilt *Himantopus himantopus* **KTU 38 cm**

Male *Immature*

D. Richards D. Richards

A distinctive black and white wader with *long red legs, a very long, slender, black bill and red eyes*. Sexes are similar but female has a blackish-brown back and wings and outside of the breeding season the head and nape are washed grey. Immature has brown wings and back. Found in pairs or in small groups, mostly inland on both soda and fresh-water lakes. Feeds by wading through deep water, sweeping its bill over the surface to obtain food items (typically insects and molluscs).

Pied Avocet *Recurvirostra avosetta* **KTU 43 cm**

G. Langsbury

Adult

An unmistakable black and white wading bird with *a long, thin, upturned bill and blue-grey legs*. Sexes are alike, and immature is brownish and white. When feeding sweeps its bill from side to side, and occasionally feeds by swimming in deeper water. Usually occurs in pairs or in small loose flocks in both soda and fresh-water lakes. Although there is apparently only a small breeding population, there is no evidence of Palaearctic birds occurring in East Africa.

54

Spotted Thick-knee *Burhinus capensis* **KTU 43 cm**

Adult

A brown plover-like bird with a large head and *large yellow eyes.* The upperparts are mottled brown, giving a *spotted appearance*, and the underparts are paler and streaked, especially on the breast. Sexes are alike, and immature is similar to adult but more streaked. Spotted Thick-knees feed in the early evening, at night and in the early morning and occur in dry rocky scrub and bush country. During the day they can be found resting in the shade of bushes and trees.

Water Thick-knee *Burhinus vermiculatus* **KTU 37 cm**

Smaller and greyer than the Spotted Thick-knee but better distinguished by the presence of a prominent *black-edged, pale grey wing bar*. Sexes are alike, and immature resembles adult. *Always found near water* (riverbanks, lake shores, beaches, estuaries and mangrove swamps) singly or in small groups, and spends the day sitting in any available waterside shade. Like the Spotted Thick-knee, it is mainly nocturnal. When disturbed, it is often reluctant to fly, usually running away from an intruder with its head held low, before finally taking to flight.

Adult

55

Two-banded Courser (Double-banded Courser) *Rhinoptilus africanus* **KTU 20 cm**

D. Richards

Adult

A small, brown, long-legged bird with very short toes, large eyes and a *distinctive upright stance.* The underparts are paler with two characteristic *black bands across the chest.* Sexes are similar and immature resembles adult. *When disturbed the bird runs* in preference to flying. In flight the wings have a distinctive rufous appearance and the black uppertail coverts are conspicuous. Occurs in small loose groups in arid grasslands and in semi-desert country.

Collared Pratincole (Red-winged Pratincole) *Glareola pratincola* **KTU 25 cm**

D. Richards

Adult

A brown, *short-legged* bird with a *white rump* and a deeply forked tail. The bill is black with a red base, and the throat is buffy edged with a thin black band. In flight the *long pointed wings* with a chestnut patch and the forked tail are conspicuous. Sexes are alike, and immature is paler than adult. Occurs in flocks in open areas around lakes, swamps and dams. The very similar Black-winged Pratincole, *G. nordmanni*, (not illustrated) has black (not rufous) underwing coverts.

Grey-headed Gull *Larus cirrocephalus* **KTU** **40 cm**

A distinctive gull with a *pale grey head, a bright red bill* and red legs. The wings are grey with black tips. Outside the breeding season the head is a much paler grey and there is a grey spot behind each ear. Sexes are similar, but immature has greyish-brown wings and a whitish head with a sooty mark behind each eye; the bill and the feet are black. A common gull, occurring on inland lakes, both fresh and alkaline. Immature and non-breeding birds may be confused with the smaller migrant Black-headed Gull, *L. ridibundus* (not illustrated) but they differ by having pale eyes, darker underwings and more black colouring on the wing tips.

Adult

D. Richards

White-winged Tern *Chlidonias leucopterus* **KTU** **24 cm**

Non-breeding adult

SIL / N. Dennis

A common migrant, usually seen in non-breeding plumage. Except for the white forehead, the head is grey-black with a dark spot in front of the eyes. The wings and back are grey, and rest of body (including rump) is white. Immature is browner than adult with a broad white collar. Best separated from similar Whiskered Tern, *C. hybridus*, (not illustrated) in flight by *white rump and contrasting grey upperparts and wings*. Occurs in large flocks on inland lakes, both fresh and alkaline.

57

Gull-billed Tern *Sterna nilotica* **KTU 38 cm**

Adult

D. Richards

A thickset tern with a distinctive *stout black bill*, pale grey upperparts with a *black cap*, and white underparts. The legs and feet are black. Sexes are alike, and immature resembles adult but shows a greyish cap. A common visitor to East Africa from mid-August to mid-April, and found most often at inland waters, both fresh and alkaline. Also occurs in large flocks over the East African plains where it feeds on flying insects and emerging dung beetles.

Black-faced Sandgrouse *Pterocles decoratus* **KTU 28 cm**

Male

D. Richards

Female

D. Richards

A small sandgrouse with a distinctive *black pattern on the face*. The upperparts are brown barred with black, the neck and chest are brown, and a narrow black line separates the chest from the white belly. The remaining underparts are black. Female lacks black face pattern of male and shows a buff, not white, belly. Immature resembles female. Occurs in dry bush and semi-desert country in pairs or in small flocks, and is most often seen in the early mornings flying to water. The similar but much rarer Lichtenstein's Sandgrouse, *S. lichtensteinii*, (not illustrated) lacks a black throat and a white belly, and has a more spotted appearance than Black-faced Sandgrouse.

Chestnut-bellied Sandgrouse *Pterocles exustus* KTU 30 cm

A yellowish-brown sandgrouse with distinctive *long, pointed central tail feathers*. These long feathers are easily visible in flight and should avoid confusion with any other sandgrouse in the region. Male has a thin black line across the chest and a dark belly. Female is darker than male with upperparts streaked and barred, and lacks the black chest line. Immature resembles female. A common bird of semi-desert and arid plains, and most often seen flying to water in the mornings or late afternoons. Usually circles a waterhole before landing a short distance away from it. When disturbed it has a habit of slowly creeping away before taking to flight.

Male

R.S. Daniell

Female

D. Richards

Speckled Pigeon *Columba guinea* KTU 41 cm

Adult

D. Richards

A large, blue-grey and chestnut pigeon with white-spotted wings. The *large red patch of bare skin around the eyes and the dark red legs* are diagnostic. Sexes are similar, and immature resembles adult but is grey where adult is brown and has brown bare skin around the eyes. Commonly found in towns and villages and in open and rocky country. The similar sized Olive Pigeon, *C. arquatrix*, (not illustrated) is darker, has a yellow bill and yellow legs, and is a forest species.

59

Namaqua Dove *Oena capensis* **KTU 21 cm**

Male

Africa's smallest dove although its characteristic long, pointed tail gives a greater length measurement than in other small doves. Male is brownish grey above and white below, and has a *black face, throat and chest*. The bill is orange-yellow but has a red base. Female lacks black on the face and has a brown bill. Immature resembles female but is browner and more spotted. In flight, the rufous colour in the wings and the long tail render the bird unmistakable. Found in pairs in arid and semi-desert country.

Female

Ring-necked Dove (Cape Turtle Dove) *Streptopelia capicola* **KTU 25 cm**

Adult

An all-grey dove with *dark eyes* and a black collar on the hindneck. The underparts are grey graduating to almost white on the belly. In flight the *white tip and white sides of the tail* are distinctive. Sexes are similar, and immature is grey tinged with buff. Smaller than both the African Mourning Dove and the Red-eyed Dove. Widespread and common in dry thornbush and savannahs. The call, often translated as 'tell father, tell father' is one of the best-known sounds of Africa.

African Mourning Dove *Streptopelia decipiens* KTU 28 cm

Adult

A pale grey dove with a black collar on the hindneck. The underparts have a pink wash to them which distinguishes the bird from the Ring-necked Dove, as does the *red bare skin around the yellow, not dark, eyes*. Also, the black collar is edged with white and *only the tops of the tail show white in flight*. Utters a very distinctive 'garoow' call. Sexes are alike, and immature is browner than adult. Found in acacia woodland, often near water at low altitudes.

Red-eyed Dove *Streptopelia semitorquata* KTU 30 cm

The largest of the grey doves, this species has a conspicuous, very *pale forehead* and a pinkish neck and underparts. The *eyes are red* surrounded by a vinous-red eye-ring and there is no white in the tail. Sexes are similar, and immature resembles adult but is duller. Generally occurs at higher altitudes than the similar Mourning Dove, in woodlands and forest edges but is also common along the coast. A common garden bird in Nairobi. Further distinguished from Mourning Dove by its red, not yellow, eyes. Ring-necked Dove is smaller and shows distinctive white in the tail.

Adult

61

Laughing Dove *Steptopelia senegalensis* **KTU 24 cm**

Adult

A small, pinkish-grey dove with *no black hindneck collar*. The wings are bluish and brown, and there are distinct black speckles on the breast. The *eyes are black encircled by a thin pink eye-ring*. In flight the white tail tips are conspicuous. Sexes are similar, and immature resembles adult but is paler. Occurs either singly or in pairs in thornbush and acacia woodlands, and is often found in and around town and villages. Utters a distinctive 'co co co co' call.

Emerald-spotted Wood-Dove *Turtur chalcospilos* **KTU 20 cm**

Adult

A small, inconspicuous, ground-living dove with a grey head and neck, a paler belly and a red bill with a black base. The upperparts are brown with *metallic-green wing spots*. When flushed typically flies a short distance before settling. In flight the rufous wing patches and two bands across the rump are conspicuous. Sexes are alike, and immature is browner in colour. The call is a distinctive, low 'du du du du du du'. Occurs in savannah woodlands, thickets and coastal scrub.

Fischer's Lovebird *Agapornis fishceri* **KT 14 cm**

Adults

D. Richards

A small, mainly green bird with a red forehead, a red bill and a white eye-ring. The cheeks and throat are orange, merging to brownish yellow on the crown. The uppertail coverts are blue. Sexes are alike, and immature is similar to adult but duller. Occurs in noisy flocks in dry acacia country. Introduced to Nairobi, Mombasa and Naivasha, where it hybridises with the Yellow-collared Lovebird and is often kept as a cage bird. Occurs naturally in northwest Tanzania.

Yellow-collared Lovebird *Agapornis personata* **KT 15 cm**

Adults

D. Richards

A mainly green bird with a *dark brown head*, a red bill and a white eye-ring. *A yellow chest band continues around the neck to form a distinctive collar.* The uppertail coverts are green. Sexes are alike, and immature resembles adult but is duller. A noisy species, usually occurring in flocks in grasslands and open woodland, especially near baobab trees. Occurs naturally in Tanzania, but introduced into Kenya where it now hybridises with Fischer's Lovebird.

Brown Parrot *Poicephalus meyeri* **KTU 25 cm**

Adult

A mainly brown parrot with a conspicuous *yellow crown and yellow shoulders*. The back and rump are green-blue, the underparts are green, and the eyes are dull red. Sexes are alike, and immature is similar to adult but lacks any yellow colouring. Occurs in pairs or small family parties in savannah woodlands. Brown-headed Parrot, *P. cryptoxanthus*, (not illustrated) has a brown head and green wings with a bright yellow underwing (Brown Parrot has only the forewing yellow).

African Orange-bellied Parrot *Poicephalus rufiventris* **KT 25 cm**

Male

The *orange breast and belly* of the male is distinctive. The upperparts are ashy-brown with a green-blue rump and the undertail coverts are green. Female is less distinctive, lacking the orange of the male, and having both the breast and the belly green. Immature resembles female. This is the characteristic parrot of dry thornbush country, and it is particularly partial to baobab trees. It occurs in pairs or small family parties but apparently never in flocks.

64

Great Blue Turaco *Corythaeola cristata* KTU 71 – 76 cm

Adult

R.S. Daniell

Unmistakable, the largest turaco in East Africa. The *blue head with its distinctive blackish-blue crest, and the yellow bill with a red tip* are diagnostic. The upperparts are blue, the breast is green merging into yellow, and the belly is chestnut. There is a black band at the end of the very long greenish-yellow tail. Sexes are alike, and immature resembles adult but is duller. Gregarious, occurring in forests where its distinctive call and habit of flopping from tree to tree makes it very conspicuous.

White-bellied Go-away-bird *Corythaixoides leucogaster* KTU 51 cm

Adult

D. Richards

A distinctive, slim-looking, *grey turaco with a white belly, a pronounced crest and a long tail.* The wings are grey with black bars and black tips, and the bill is brownish but during the breeding season turns to green. Sexes are alike, and immature is similar to adult but is browner in colour. Occurs in small flocks in hot, dry thornbush country where the birds typically announce themselves by their well-known, drawn-out 'wah wah wah' call.

Eastern Grey Plantain-eater *Crinifer zonurus* KTU 51 cm

Adult

R.S. Daniell

A mainly greyish-brown turaco, its white-tipped feathers on the nape and hindneck form a shaggy crest. The bill is yellow-green. In flight a *white bar* is noticeable *in the wings.* Sexes are alike, and immature resembles the adult but lacks a crest. *A very noisy* species with a strange chuckling call. Occurs in savannah woodland, cultivated areas and riverine vegetation, and it is partial to figs. Occurs up to 1 800 m, and is particularly common around Lake Victoria. Should not be confused with the Bare-faced Go-away-bird, *Corythaixoides personata*, (not illustrated) which has a distinctive black face and a white neck.

Hartlaub's Turaco *Tauraco hartlaubi* KTU 41 cm

D. Richards

Adult

A mainly green turaco with a rounded, blue-black crest and a distinctive Africa-shaped *white patch above and in front of the eyes*. The eyes are encircled by a coral-red ring, and the bill is green. The wings have red tips and the tail is dark violet-blue. *In flight the crimson colouring in the wings* is conspicuous. Sexes are alike, and immature resembles adult but is duller. Common in highland forests where it draws attention to itself by its loud calls.

Diederik Cuckoo *Chrysococcyx caprius* KTU 19 cm

Male

Common and often conspicuous, with a well-known *'dee-dee-dee-deedric' call*. The upperparts are metallic green with a coppery wash, and there are *white blotches on the wing*. The underparts are white with coppery-green bars on the blanks. The *white eye-stripe, red eyes and black bill* are distinctive. Female is more coppery on the back and wings and has coppery flank bars. Occurs mainly in thornbush and acacia country, often near weaver colonies – which it parasitises. The similar Klaas' Cuckoo, *C. klaas*, (not illustrated) lacks white spots on the wing, is greener above, whiter below and has dark eyes. Female Klaas' Cuckoo differs by being finely barred below.

Red-chested Cuckoo *Cuculus solitarius* KTU 31 cm

A common cuckoo, but heard far more often than it is seen. The *upperparts are dark blue-grey* and the underparts are buffy-white finely barred black and with a *rufous throat and upper breast*. Sexes are similar, and immature is darker than the adult with a blackish throat and a barred white belly. A tree-top bird found in a variety of habitats, from gardens and woodlands to forest and bush, where its well-known, persistent call rendered as 'it-will-rain', is a feature during the rainy season. This cuckoo parasitises the Cape Robin-Chat (p. 93) and also various thrushes.

Adult

D. Richards

White-browed Coucal *Centropus superciliosus* KTU 41 cm

Adult

A large, clumsy-looking bird with a *black cap and chestnut wings*, and a long black tail. The *white eye-stripe*, pale streaks on the nape and the deep red eyes are distinctive. The underparts are buffy-white and the flanks are finely streaked. Sexes are alike, and immature is similar to adult but has browner underparts and a brown (rather than white) eye-stripe. Found in coastal scrub and rank grass and bush, where its well-known bubbly call – likened to water being poured out of a bottle and accounting for its popular name of the 'Water Bottle Bird' – is commonly heard. A skulking bird, often seen walking on the ground.

Spotted Eagle-Owl *Bubo africanus* KTU 51 cm

Adult

Occurs in two colour phases, a greyish form and a brown form. Both forms have finely barred upperparts and show dark spotting on the breast. The *large ear tufts and bright yellow eyes* are diagnostic. Sexes are alike, and immature is browner than the adult with less spotting. Usually found in pairs, this owl occurs in dry bush country, in rocky ravines, on kopjes and often on buildings (for example, in safari lodges). The similar Greyish-Eagle Owl, *Bubo cinerascens*, which occurs in Northern Kenya, has dark eyes. A race of this owl, Mackinder's Eagle Owl *(B.a. mackinderi)* is larger and has orange eyes.

Verreaux's Eagle-Owl (Giant Eagle-Owl) *Bubo lacteus* **KTU 61 – 66 cm**

Larger than the Spotted Eagle-Owl and generally grey in colour, finely vermiculated brown, the face is distinctly paler and is edged with black, the eyes are dark with *conspicuous pink eyelids, and the bill is white*. The *ear tufts are small and not always visible*. Sexes are alike but female is larger than male. Immature resembles adult but is browner. Occurs in acacia woodland and bush, and in savannah country, often along rivers and water courses; also found in cultivated country. Prefers large trees where it typically roosts on a large branch in deep shade. The bird's *call, a deep low 'hu hu-hu hoo'*, is often heard – both during the day and at night.

Adult

D. Richards

Pearl-spotted Owlet *Glaucidium perlatum* **KTU 20 cm**

Adult

D. Richards

A small owl with a *longish, white-spotted, black tail*. The upperparts are rich brown spotted with white, and the underparts are white with dark brown streaks. The bill and eyes are yellow, and it has *distinctive dark marks (false eyes) on the back of the head*. Sexes are alike, and immature resembles adult. Often seen during the day, at times being mobbed by other birds. Occurs in dry acacia bush country. The call is distinctive: a series of 'pwee pwee pwee' notes, rising in volume.

69

Montane Nightjar *Caprimulgus poliocephalus* **KTU 24 cm**

D. Richards

Adult

A dusky brown nightjar, best identified by its distinctive plaintive call ('pee-ee pee-ee'). It has a *rufous collar on the hindneck* which is diagnostic. *In flight the two white patches on the wings and the two white outer tail feathers* are distinctive, the latter serving to distinguish it from most other nightjars in the region. Sexes are similar but female differs in having the wing patches buffy not white. Found in the highlands in woodlands, wooded gardens and along forest edges.

Little Swift *Apus affinis* **KTU 13 cm**

R.S. Daniell

Adult

A small black swift with a white rump, a white chin and square tail. Sexes are alike, and immature resembles adult but is duller. A colonial species occurring in noisy flocks, it breeds on buildings and bridges in cities and towns. The similar White-rumped Swift, *A. caffer*, (not illustrated) has less white on the rump and a distinctive forked tail. The Horus Swift, *A. horus*, (not illustrated) is larger, more thickset and has the white on the throat extending on to the chest and forehead.

African Palm Swift *Cypsiurus parvus* KTU 13 cm

This small and slim-bodied brown swift has slender wings and a deeply forked tail. In flight the tail is more often held closed, forming a sharp point. Sexes are alike and immature resembles adult but has a shorter tail. A widespread resident swift, it is always associated with tall palm trees, where it nests – using its saliva to glue both nest material and its eggs to the inside of vertical, hanging palm leaves. The similar Scarce Swift, *Schoutedenapus myoptilus*, (not illustrated) is a larger bird, has a greyish-brown throat, and is a highland species, not normally associated with palms but preferring rocky crags for nesting.

Adult

P.J. Ginn

Speckled Mousebird *Colius striatus* KTU 33 cm

A generally brown bird with a very long tail and a distinctive head crest. The body feathers are edged with white, imparting a speckled appearance (hence its common name). The face is black with white cheek patches, and the legs are red. Sexes are alike, and immature is similar to adult but has a short tail and a pale bill (adult's bill is dark). A gregarious species, occurring in woodlands, scrub and cultivated areas. The White-headed Mousebird, *C. leucocepahlus*, is similar but has a distinctive white head and barred underparts, and occurs in dry bush country.

Adults

D. Richards

71

Blue-naped Mousebird *Urocolius macrourus* **KTU 36 cm**

Adult

An ash-grey mousebird, longer and slimmer than the Speckled Mousebird (p. 71), and with a *distinctive turquoise-blue patch on the nape and a long, slender, pointed tail*. The face is bright red as is the base of the bill, and the feet are dull red. Sexes are alike, and immature is paler than adult and lacks the blue colouring on the nape. These birds fly fast in small parties, uttering their very distinctive 'peee-peee' call. They are found in open dry bush country below 1 900 m.

Pied Kingfisher *Ceryle rudis* **KTU 25 cm**

Male (left) *and female* (right)

A distinctive *black and white kingfisher with a crested head and very long bill.* The male has two black bands across the chest, and the female has one incomplete black chest band. Commonly *hunts by hovering* before diving, beak first, into water. Will readily use perches, even telephone lines or boats, if available. Occurs at most inland waters and also at the coast. Usually found singly or in pairs, occasionally gregarious, and at times very noisy.

D. Richards

D. Richards

Malachite Kingfisher *Alcedo cristata* **KTU 14 cm**

This tiny kingfisher has a large red bill, a *green-blue crest* and red feet. The upperparts are ultramarine and there is a distinctive white patch on the side of the neck. The underparts are rufous and the throat is white. Sexes are alike, and immature is duller than adult and has a black bill. *Found at almost any permanent fresh water with fringing vegetation.* The similar Pygmy Kingfisher, *Ispidina picta*, (not illustrated) lacks a crest and has an ultramarine head and violet-coloured cheeks; also, it occurs in woodland habitats. Immature Malachite Kingfisher is often mistaken for the much larger Half-collared Kingfisher, *A. semitorquata*, (not illustrated).

Adult

D. Richards

Striped Kingfisher *Halcyon chelicuti* **KTU 17cm**

This *small dull-coloured kingfisher has a dark, streaky head,* a black eye-stripe, a distinctive *buffy-white collar, and a red and black bill.* The rump and tail are azure-blue, seen clearly in flight only. Sexes are alike, and immature resembles adult but is duller. The bird's loud, trilling call is a feature of its woodland and savannah country habitat. Feeds on insects, grasshoppers and lizards. Often sits in a hunched position on an open branch. The Brown-hooded Kingfisher, *H. albiventris*, (not illustrated) is larger, has an all-red bill and a paler head.

Adult

D. Richards

73

Grey-headed Kingfisher *Halcyon leucocephala* KTU 20 cm

An insect-eating kingfisher with a distinctive *rich chestnut belly,* cobalt-blue wings and a cobalt-blue tail. The head is grey or grey-brown and the bill and feet are bright red. Sexes are alike and immature resembles adult but is duller. Immature birds, in particular, but also the adults, may be confused with the Brown-hooded Kingfisher, *H. albiventris,* (not illustrated) but that species lacks a chestnut belly. The Grey-headed Kingfisher occurs singly or in pairs in savannah and wooded country, and often along water courses, where it feeds on a variety of insects and small lizards, although never fish.

D. Richards

Adult

Woodland Kingfisher *Halcyon senegalensis* KTU 20 cm

This distinctive, mainly *bright-blue kingfisher has a large bill with a red upper mandible and a black lower mandible.* The upperparts are blue-grey, the underparts are whitish, and it has black feet. The wings, back and tail are blue and the shoulders are black. Sexes are alike, and immature is similar to adult but is duller. Occurs in savannah country and woodland with scattered trees, where it feeds on a variety of insects, frogs and, at times, fish. The call is a loud distinctive trill. The similar Mangrove Kingfisher, *H. senegaloides,* (not illustrated) is confined to coastal areas.

D. Richards

Adult

White-throated Bee-eater *Merops albicollis* **KTU 28 cm**

A distinctive slim bee-eater with a *long thin tail*. It has a *black crown, eye-stripe and chest band, all of which contrast strongly with the white throat and forehead.* The rest of the plumage is pale green becoming paler on the belly. In flight or when the male is displaying it shows *conspicuous cinnamon colouring in the wings.* Sexes are similar although female has a shorter tail than the male. Immature is duller than adult and has a short tail. Occurs in savannah and dry semi-desert country where it is gregarious, especially during the breeding season. These bee-eaters often excavate their nest holes in flat, bare ground.

Adult

D. Richards

European Bee-eater *Merops apiaster* **KTU 28 cm**

A mainly *blue and green bee-eater.* The *head and upper back are rich chestnut* in colour, the lower back is gold and the throat is *bright yellow.* Sexes are alike, and immature is duller than adult and has a green-brown back. Mainly a passage migrant to East Africa, passing through from September to November and again during March and April, although some do winter in the area, mostly in Tanzania. Usually seen in small groups, gracefully hawking insects high in the sky (when distinctive rufous-coloured wings can be seen), and uttering their characteristic liquid call.

Adult

D. Richards

White-fronted Bee-eater *Merops bullockoides* KT 23 cm

D. Richards

Adult

The *bright red throat contrasting with the white forehead and white chin,* and the broad black band through the eye of this bee-eater are distinctive. The remaining underparts are cinnamon, the upperparts are mainly green, and the head and neck are golden-brown. The deep blue undertail coverts are best seen in flight. Sexes are alike, and immature is similar to adult but is duller. Common in the Rift Valley in Kenya, and often found along dry watercourses where it breeds colonially, in sandy banks and cliffs. Very noisy around its nesting areas, where its characteristic loud 'waark, waark' call is a common feature.

Northern Carmine Bee-eater *Merops nubicus* KTU 38 cm

D. Richards

Adult

This large, unmistakable *carmine-red bee-eater has a long, pointed tail. The head and throat are dark blue-green* and the rump is light blue. Sexes are alike, and immature is similar to adult but is duller and has a shorter tail. Gregarious, especially at roosts along the East African coast (where it is common) from November to March. Also often seen perched on roadside telephone wires. Breeds in colonies in the Lake Turkana area in Kenya. The similar Southern Carmine Bee-eater, *M. nubicoides,* (not illustrated) differs by having a red throat.

76

Cinnamon-chested Bee-eater *Merops oreobates* **KTU 22 cm**

A common resident *highland* bee-eater with *deep green upperparts, a yellow throat, a conspicuous white cheek spot* and a black gorget. There is a distinctive black band through the eye. Sexes are alike, and immature is greenish in colour, generally duller than the adult and lacks a black gorget. Occurs in pairs or small groups, especially when breeding, along forest edges and clearings. Often common in suburban garden in Nairobi. May be confused with the Little Bee-eater but that species is much smaller, has a distinctive blue line above the eye, and occurs at lower altitudes and in different habitats to this species.

Adult

R.S. Daniell

Little Bee-eater *Merops pusillus* **KTU 17 cm**

This, the smallest and commonest bee-eater is mainly green with a bright yellow throat and a black gorget which has a thin blue line along its upper edge. A distinctive *bright blue line above the eye* borders a broad black eye-band. The upper chest is chestnut becoming paler below. Sexes are alike, and immature is duller than the adult, lacks a black gorget, and has a greenish, not chestnut, chest. Usually *occurs in pairs in open grasslands or along the shores of lakes and swamps. Habitually perches on low bushes or on rocks* from where it hawks insects.

Adult

D. Richards

77

Lilac-breasted Roller *Coracias caudata* KTU 41 cm

Adult

A common species occurring in almost all national parks and reserves, and in some areas a common roadside bird. The *lilac throat and breast, and elongated outer tail feathers are distinctive*. Perches on open branches, large termite mounds and even on power and telephone lines, swooping down on its prey and clearly showing its brilliant blue wings. Sexes are alike, and immature is duller than adult and lacks the long outer tail feathers. Occurs in thornbush, savannahs and in open woodland. The Abyssinian Roller, *C. abyssinica*, (not illustrated) is similar but lacks the distinctive lilac breast and throat of this species.

D. Richards

European Roller *Coracias garrulus* KTU 31 cm

D. Richards

Adult

A migrant from eastern Europe and Asia, visiting the region from October to April and very conspicuous on its return migration in March/April. The adult is unmistakable with it *bright blue head, throat, belly and wings*, its brown back and its short tail. Sexes are alike, and immature is paler than adult and may be confused with Lilac-breasted Roller but its pale throat and chest distinguish it. Occurs in similar habitats to the Lilac-breasted Roller.

African Hoopoe *Upupa africana* KTU 28 cm

Adult

An unmistakable, fairly common bird, generally cinnamon-rufous in colour with contrasting black and white wings and tail. Feeds on the ground, probing with its long, decurved black bill. Raises its distinctive black-tipped, fan-shaped crest when alarmed. Its undulating flight is distinctive, during which the black and white wings are conspicuous. Frequents grasslands and open woodlands, where its characteristic, soft, low, 'hoo-poo-poo' call is a feature.

Green Wood-hoopoe (Red-billed Wood-hoopoe) *Phoeniculus purpureus* KTU 38 – 41 cm

A black-looking bird with a green-blue gloss and a long graduated tail. It has a conspicuous, long, curved, red bill and red legs. In flight the white wing bar and white tips to the tail feathers are noticeable. Common in woodlands where it occurs in noisy parties, climbing about tree trunks and branches. Sexes are similar but female is smaller than the male and has a shorter bill. Immature is duller overall and has a short, curved, black bill. May be confused with the Common Scimitarbill, *P. cyanomelas*, (not illustrated) but that bird has a slender, curved, black (not red) bill.

Adult

Silvery-cheeked Hornbill *Bycanistes brevis* **KT 66 – 74 cm**

A large, mainly black hornbill with a white lower back and rump, a white belly and white tips to the tail feathers. Male is distinguished by the large horn-coloured casque, the faint pale line at the base of its brown bill, the blue bare skin around the red eyes, and the silvery-tipped facial feathers. Female is smaller than male and lacks the large casque. Immature has a smaller bill and brown-edged facial feathers. A forest hornbill, found in pairs or small parties east of the Kenya/Tanzania Rift Valley. Common when fig trees are fruiting, when

Female (left) *and male* (right)

the birds enter towns, drawing attention to themselves with their loud baying calls.

D. Richards

Black-and-white casqued Hornbill *Bycanistes subcylindricus* **KTU 69 – 76 cm**

A large, mainly black hornbill, distinguished from the Silvery-cheeked Hornbill by the *large white patch in the wings (conspicuous in flight)* and by its black and white casque. Female is smaller than male and has a much reduced (almost absent) casque. Immature has a small bill and lacks a casque. A forest species found in the western parts of East Africa. The smaller Trumpeter Hornbill, *B. bucinator*, (not illustrated) differs from this and the Silvery-cheeked Hornbill by its white lower chest and belly and by its habitat choice (riverine forest and scrub in coastal areas).

Male

R.S. Daniell

80

Crowned Hornbill *Tockus alboterminatus* KTU 48 – 51 cm

The slim mainly *blackish-brown hornbill has a dusky red bill and casque*. The lower chest and belly are white, as are the outer tips of the tail feathers. A small head crest is sometimes visible. The sides of the head and the nape are streaked white and there is a pale, sometimes indistinct yellowish band at the base of the bill. Female is smaller than male and lacks a casque. Immature is duller than adult and has an orange-yellow bill. Found mostly in pairs in forests and woodlands, its piping call and buoyant flight are distinctive. Hemprich's

Male

Hornbill, *T. hemprichii,* (not illustrated) is a similar but uncommon species, confined to dry, rocky country.

Van der Decken's Hornbill *Tockus deckeni* KT 43 – 51 cm

Male

Female

A distinctive *black and white hornbill with an ivory-tipped red bill* and conspicuous *pink-coloured throat patches*. The face and underparts are white and contrast with the black wings. Female resembles male but is smaller and has a black bill. Immature is similar to adults but has a shorter, blackish bill. Usually found in pairs (often feeding on the ground) in semi-arid savannah country. The similar Jackson's Hornbill, *T. jacksoni* (not illustrated) has white-spotted wing coverts.

Red-billed Hornbill *Tockus erythrorhynchus* KTU 43 – 46 cm

Adult

The slender, *all-red bill and white-spotted black wings* render this hornbill unmistakable. Female is similar to male but is smaller and has a smaller bill. Immature resembles adult but has a much shorter, brownish-coloured bill. A common species, it is usually seen in pairs feeding on the ground on insects, seeds and scorpions. Occurs in semi-arid savannahs and thornbush country where its monotonous 'kok kok kok' call is a characteristic feature.

Eastern Yellow-billed Hornbill *Tockus flavirostris* KTU 46 – 53 cm

Adult

Similar to the Red-billed Hornbill, but *larger and with a distinctive large yellow, not red, bill.* The two pink-coloured patches of bare skin on the throat and the *yellow eyes* are also diagnostic. Sexes are similar but female is smaller than male and has black, not pink, bare skin throat patches. Immature is similar to adult but has a shorter, pale-yellow bill. Frequents dry thornbush country, and typically feeds on the ground where it has a special relationship with the dwarf mongoose, feeding on insects flushed by the animals and in turn warning them of avian predators.

82

Southern Ground Hornbill *Bucorvus leadbeateri* KTU 107 cm

D. Richards

Male

An unmistakable black *turkey-sized bird with a large black bill and distinctive red bare skin on the face and throat.* Female has an additional small blue patch of bare skin below the bill. Immature is brownish black in colour and has a shorter bill. Usually found in pairs or small family parties, *walking through open country.* Flies rarely, but when it does the *white primaries are conspicuous.* Male's booming call, 'ho ho ho', is followed by a slightly higher 'hu hu hu', given by the female.

Yellow-rumped Tinkerbird *Pogoniulus bilineatus* KTU 10 cm

D. Richards

Adult

A small, *black and white bird with distinctive white stripes above and below the eyes.* When seen at close quarters the yellow wash on the belly, yellow edges to the wing feathers, and bright orange-yellow rump can be seen. Sexes are similar, and immature resembles adults but is duller overall. A common species, inhabiting forests, and often difficult to see. The *call, 'tok tok tok',* uttered in a series of short bursts, is a characteristic sound of its forest habitat.

d'Arnaud's Barbet *Trachyphonus darnaudii* KTU 16 cm

Adult

A mainly yellowish-brown barbet with a *yellowish head marked with black spots*. The wings and back are brown, spotted with white and it has a white-spotted black tail. There is a black patch in the centre of the throat and the undertail coverts are bright red. Sexes are alike, and immature is similar to adults. The birds' *display is distinctive: a male and female sit opposite each other, swinging their tails in an almost mechanical way, and at the same time uttering their duetting call* 'doo doo dee dok, doo doo dee dok' over and over again. Occurs in dry bush country and wooded grassland where it is widespread and can be common.

Red-and-yellow Barbet *Trachyphonus erythrocephalus* KTU 23 cm

Female

A very distinctive *red and yellow bird with large red bill* and a black crown. The wings and tail are black, spotted with white and yellow. The underparts are yellow with an orange wash on the chest, and there is a spotted, black and white chest band and a black streak down the throat. Female is similar to male but lacks the black throat streak, and has a red crown tipped with black. Immature is paler than adult. Common in semi-arid bush country. Favours termite mounds in which it often nests. The call, which sounds like 'red and yellow', is uttered repeatedly and in duet.

D. Richards

84

Greater Honeyguide *Indicator indicator* **KTU 20 cm**

Immature　　　　　*Male*

R.S. Daniell　　　　　P.J. Ginn

A distinctive bird with a *stout, bright pink bill, white cheek patches and a black throat*. The upperparts are greyish brown, and the underparts are buffy. In flight, the *white outer tail feathers are conspicuous*. Female is duller than the male, has a pale bill, and lacks the black throat and white cheek patches. Immature has a brown head and back and yellowish underparts. Common in various habitats except for very arid areas. Utters a characteristic call: 'weet purr, weet purr'.

Nubian Woodpecker *Campethera nubica* **KTU 18 cm**

The green-brown upperparts of this bird are spotted and barred yellowish. The tail feathers are barred yellow and brown and have distinctive yellow shafts. The *underparts are buffy white with dark spots which become streaks on the flanks*. Male has a red moustachial stripe; female has a white-spotted black crown and a small red patch on the nape. Common, and often seen in pairs in open woodland and savannahs. The very similar Golden-tailed Woodpecker, *C. abingoni*, (not illustrated) is green and has streaks, not spots, on the underparts.

D. Richards

Male

85

Grey Woodpecker *Mesopicos goertae* KTU 18 cm

A distinctive wood-pecker with *grey head and under-parts, green wings and back*, and a brown tail with yellowish bars. The rump is red, as is the lower belly and undertail coverts. *Male has a red patch on the rear of the crown, which extends on to the nape.* Female lacks any red on the head, and immature resembles the adult but is greener and has the red colouring more diffused. Common along forest edges and in acacia woodland from 700 m to 2 000 m. The Olive Wood-pecker, *M. griseocephalus*, (not illustrated) is similar but can be distinguished by its olive, not grey breast; also, it is found in highland forests up to 3 700 m.

R.S. Daniell

Female

Red-capped Lark *Calandrella cinerea* KTU 14 cm

A small, rich-brown lark with a distinctive *chestnut cap*. The underparts are pale with chestnut patches on each side of the chest. Sexes are alike, and immature resembles the adult but lacks the chest-nut cap. *In flight, the white outer tail feathers are visible and the dark tail contrasts with the rufous rump.* Common, often in flocks, in open plains and cultivated fields. The Fawn-coloured Lark, *Mirafra africanoides*, (not illustrated) is similar in size but occurs at lower altitudes, lacks the chest-nut cap and chest patches and has a distinctive white eye-stripe.

R.S. Daniell

Adult

86

Rufous-naped Lark *Mirafra africana* **KTU** **18 cm**

A common, sturdy, short-tailed lark with a heavy bill and a short crest. The upperparts are rich brown, and the wings are brown with *red primaries, which are very conspicuous in flight.* The rufous nape is often absent, particularly in birds found in Kenya. The underparts are pale with black streaks on the chest and flanks. Sexes are alike. The bird's call is characteristic, comprising three to four sweet musical notes delivered from the top of a small bush, rock or termite mound. Occurs in open plains and bushed grasslands. The very similar Red-winged Bush Lark, *M. hypermetra*, (not illustrated) is larger and has a noticeably longer tail.

Adult

Lesser Striped Swallow *Hirundo abyssinica* **KTU** **18 cm**

Adults

A distinctive swallow with *heavily streaked underparts, a bright chestnut crown and rump, and a deeply forked tail.* The rest of the upperparts are dark glossy blue. Sexes are alike, and immature is similar to adult but has a browish-black crown, a buffy breast and a shorter tail. Frequents a variety of habitats, from grassland to forest edge; often seen nesting under the eaves of houses and under bridges.

87

Barn (European) Swallow *Hirundo rustica* KTU 18 cm

Adult

R.S. Daniell

A common and well-known migrant bird, often occurring in large flocks from September to April. The upperparts are blue-black, and the face and throat are red. The *underparts are white or buffy, and there is a dark band below the throat*. Sexes are similar, both male and female showing *long tail streamers*. Immature is much paler than adult and lacks long outer tail feathers. The Angola Swallow, *H. angolensis*, (not illustrated) is similar but smaller, has grey underparts and shorter outer tail feathers; immature Barn Swallow may be confused with that species but is distinguished by the fact that it is always much paler.

Wire-tailed Swallow *Hirundo smithii* KTU 15 cm

Adult

D. Richards

The distinctive *long, thin, outer tail feathers* of this bird are sometimes difficult to see – particularly in flight, which is swift. The bird's upperparts are glassy blue, the *underparts are white*, and it has a rufous crown. Sexes are alike, and immature resembles adult but is duller. Although partial to water, the bird can be found almost anywhere, except for very arid areas. Occurs in pairs and, although common, never occurs in vast numbers. The similar Ethiopian Swallow, *H. aethiopica*, (not illustrated) is also white below but has short outer tail feathers.

88

Black Saw-wing *Psalidoprocne holomelas* KTU 18 cm

A slender, *all-black swallow with a deeply forked tail.* Sexes are similar, and immature resembles adult but has a shorter tail. *The flight is distinctive, being slow and fluttering.* Usually found singly or in small loose flocks, it occurs in woodland and forest clearings, or along forest edges, mostly in the highlands where it is quite common. The male White-headed Saw-wing, *P. albiceps*, (not illustrated) is easily distinguished by its white head but the female lacks the white head and is therefore difficult to separate. The all-brown

Adult

D. Richards

African Rock Martin, *Hirundo fuligula*, (not illustrated) can be distinguished by the distinct white spots in its tail.

Fork-tailed Drongo (Common Drongo) *Dicrurus adsimilis* KTU 25 cm

A *glossy-black bird with a distinctive forked tail, bright red eyes and a strong, hook-tipped bill.* In flight the pale inner webs of the flight feathers are very noticeable. Sexes are alike, and immature is greyer than adult. A conspicuous, often noisy and aggressive bird, it perches on open branches, from which it hawks its prey. Prefers open areas in woodland, forest edges, acacia country and cultivation up to 2 000 m. The call is a harsh, sometimes grating song; also imitates other birds. Square-tailed Drongo, *D. ludwigii*, (not illustrated) is smaller and tail is only slightly forked.

Adult

D. Richards

89

African Black-headed Oriole *Oriolus larvatus* KTU 23 cm

Adult

This distinctive, *bright yellow bird has a black head and throat and a bright coral-red bill.* The wings are black, with a small white patch which is particularly visible in flight. The *eyes are red.* Sexes are alike, and immature is duller than adult and has streaking on the throat. A common species, usually found in pairs in forests and woodland, though often difficult to see as it typically feeds in the tops of trees. Best located by its distinctive call: a short, loud, far-carrying, clear whistle that falls in pitch. The Montane Oriole, *O. percivali,* (not illustrated) has black central tail feathers and is a highland forest species.

Pied Crow *Corvus albus* KTU 46 cm

Adult

A predominantly black crow with a distinctive white breast and a white collar. Sexes are alike, and immature resembles adult. Widespread and often common and gregarious, it feeds and roosts in towns and villages. The White-necked Raven, *C. albicollis,* (not illustrated) is larger and the areas of white on the body are restricted to the nape. The raven is a bird of mostly mountain and rocky areas but wanders extensively, and is often seen on the outskirts of Nairobi.

Cape Rook (Black Crow) *Corvus capensis* KTU 43 cm

This is an all-black corvid with a distinctive slender bill. Sexes are alike, and immature resembles the adults. Locally common, the Cape Rook occurs mainly in upland areas in open plains, light woodland and cultivated areas where it typically builds a large, untidy nest in a tree. Particularly common in the Lake Turkana area and also in the Rift Valley Highlands, and is thought to be spreading southwards. The all-black Fan-tailed Raven, *C. rhipidurus,* (not illustrated) is similar in size but has a much heavier bill and a short tail. Further, it

D. Richards

Adult

is an inhabitant of rocky and craggy hillsides and cliffs in arid and semi-arid country.

House Crow (Indian House Crow) *Corvus splendens* KT 42 cm

R.S. Daniell

Adult

An increasingly common, *slender-looking crow. The body is dark grey,* and the *head, wings and tail are black.* Sexes are alike, and immature resembles the adults but is duller. Introduced from India, it is now very common along the East African coast, particularly in Mombasa, Zanzibar and Dar es Salaam. In Mombasa it has become a serious pest, and is believed to be responsible for the decline of the Speckled Mousebird, Morning Thrush and Palm Weaver.

91

Rufous Chatterer *Turboides rubiginosus* KTU 20 cm

Adult

A distinctive *cinnamon and rufous bird with pale eyes and a horn-coloured bill*. Sexes are alike, and immature resembles adult but is duller. Gregarious and noisy, it occurs in small parties in thick scrub in arid areas and coastal bush. The Sealy Chatterer, *T. aylmeri*, (not illustrated) is similar but is ash-brown above and cinnamon-buff below with a buff-streaked white throat and breast imparting a scaly appearance; it is uncommon and occurs in woodland and dry bush country.

Common Bulbul (Black-eyed Bulbul) *Pycnonotus barbatus* KTU 18 cm

A common and well-known bird. The head and throat are blackish brown, the back is brown and the breast and belly are buffy white. It has distinctive *yellow under-tail coverts*. Often raises the feathers on the nape, which gives the head a crested appearance. Sexes are alike, and immature resembles the adult but is duller overall. A wide-spread bird, it occurs in pairs in almost any type of habitat; it is especially common in town and city gardens. The bird's distinctive call, a rapid 'towee-too-tweeoo', is often translated as 'come back to Calcutta'.

Adult

Spotted Morning-Thrush *Cichladusa guttata* KTU **16 cm**

A shy and skulking species with dull rufous-brown upperparts and a conspicuous rufous tail. The underparts are buffy. A line of black spots which run from the bill to the sides of the throat become larger black blobs on the breast. Sexes are alike, and immature resembles the adult but is duller. A locally common bird, found in thickets in dry bush country, especially along dry river courses; also uncommonly in coastal scrub. The call, a loud, melodious song, is usually delivered from a prominent perch at dawn and dusk, and occasionally at night as well; it also utters a harsh alarm call and is known to mimic other bird calls.

Adult

D. Richards

Cape Robin-Chat *Cossypha caffra* KTU **17 cm**

The *orange-rufous throat and upper breast of* this bird are characteristic and contrast with the grey belly. The head, back and tail are dusky, and the rump and outer tail feathers are rufous. A *distinctive white eye-stripe and a thin black streak are visible on each side of the face*. Sexes are alike, and immature is brown with mottling and spotting, and has a duller rufous tail. Has a habit of raising and lowering its tail. A shy bird, it occurs in the highlands along forest edges and in scrub, and often becomes confiding in gardens. Parasitised by the Red-chested Cuckoo (67).

Adult

D. Richards

93

White-browed Robin-Chat (Heuglin's Robin) *Cossypha heuglini* KTU **20 cm**

D. Richards

Adult

Immediately separable from Cape Robin-Chat (p. 93) by the *underparts which are entirely orange-rufous*. The head is black and separated from the greyish mantle by an orange collar. A conspicuous white eye-stripe extends from the forehead to the nape. The rump and outer tail feathers are rufous, and the *wings and central tail feathers are greyish*. Sexes are similar, and immature is brownish with buff spotting. Shy and skulking, it occurs up to 2 200 m in woodland, thickets and coastal scrub. Known for it melodious song given in early morning and afternoon.

Rüppell's Robin-Chat *Cossypha semirufa* KTU **18 cm**

D. Richards

Adult

Very difficult to separate from White-browed Robin-Chat although altitude at which it occurs may aid identification. Differs from that species by being slightly smaller, and by having a *darker mantle and wings and blackish central tail feathers*. Sexes are similar, and immature is brownish spotted with buff. Its song is a loud, three-noted whistle repeated over and over again; also an excellent mimic. Shy and skulking, it occurs in highland forests and dense scrub from 1 400 m to 3 300 m.

Northern Anteater Chat *Myrmecocichla aethiops* **KT 20 cm**

This chat is all-blackish-brown except for the *conspicuous white wing patches, visible only in flight*. Sexes are alike, and immature is brownish in colour. May be confused with the Sooty Chat, *M. nigra*, (not illustrated) but male Sooty Chat has a conspicuous white patch on the shoulder and shows no white in the wings in flight. Female Sooty Chat is all brown. The Anteater Chat occurs in open dry grasslands, often around termite mounds. It excavates a nest burrow in a termite mound, antbear

Adult

D. Richards

hole or warthog hole, or in a roadside cutting, which it uses year round both as a roost and as a nest site.

Isabelline Wheatear *Oemanthe isabellina* **KTU 16 cm**

A migrant bird from Europe and Asia, occurring in East Africa from October to March. It is overall pale sandy in colour with a pale eye-stripe and a characteristic white rump. Found in arid and semi-arid areas below 2 000 m, often in stony places and on bare ground or short grassland in open country. Sexes are similar, and immature resembles adults. May be confused with the female Northern Wheatear (p. 96), but *its pale wings and little or no contrast between the wings and the back* (seen in flight) distinguish it from that species; it is also larger and longer-legged.

Male

D. Richards

Northern (European) Wheatear *Oemanthe oemanthe* KTU 15 cm

D. Richards

Breeding male

Female

D. Richards

A migrant from Europe and Asia, seen from September to March. *Breeding male is distinctive with its grey crown and mantle, black cheeks, black wings, and pale eye-stripe*. The underparts are buffy pink. Non-breeding males are duller and have much reduced black on the cheeks. Female and immature are browner, and lack black on the cheeks. Both sexes have a characteristic white rump, and the upper part of the outer tail feathers is white, forming a 'T'. *In flight, the pale back contrasts with darker wings*. Occurs in open bush country.

Capped Wheatear *Oenanthe pileata* KTU 18 cm

A locally common, resident wheatear with a *black cap* and a characteristic *white rump*. The cheeks and breast are black, and it has a white forehead, eye-stripe and throat. The belly is white and there is a pinkish wash on the flanks. The upperparts are brown. It has a distinctive *upright stance*, and typically stands on a rock or mound from which it flutters straight upwards while singing. Sexes are similar, and immature resembles adult but is duller, with a brownish colour replacing the black of the adult. Occurs singly in short open grassland.

D. Richards

Adult

Cliff Chat (Mocking Chat) *Myrmecocihla cinnamomeiventris* **KTU 20 cm**

Male

The male is a distinctive bird with its glossy-black head, breast, back, wings and tail. The belly, rump and both the upper and lower tail coverts are rich rufous. There is a conspicuous white shoulder patch. Female is grey and rufous and lacks the white shoulder patch; immature resembles the female. Occurs in pairs on cliffs, gorges and rocky, boulder-strewn slopes. Utters a sweet warbling song. A tame and confiding species, especially in areas visited by tourists.

Female

D. Richards

Northern Olive Thrush *Turdus abyssinicus* **KTU 23 cm**

Adult

D. Richards

A common thrush with olive-brown upperparts, a paler breast and throat with dark streaking on the throat, and an *orange-rufous belly*. The bill and feet are orange-yellow and it has a striking *yellow ring around the eyes*. Sexes are alike, and immature is duller than adult. Occurs in pairs, in forests, woodlands and cultivated areas with trees; especially common in gardens in Nairobi. The call is a monotonous 'chee-chee-chee-chee', repeated over and over again.

97

Yellow-breasted Apalis *Apalis flavida* KTU 11 cm

R.S. Daniell

Adult

A *small, long-tailed bird* with green upperparts, a grey forehead and face, and *red eyes*. It is white below with a distinctive broad yellow band across the chest and a *small black mark in the centre of the chest*. Sexes are similar, and immature is duller than the adult and has a shorter tail. Occurs in pairs in woodland, forest edges and acacia scrub. Often holds its tail cocked particularly when duetting. The call is a distinctive rolling 'kreek kreek', often likened to galloping hooves.

Grey-backed Camaroptera *Camaroptera brachyura* KTU 10 cm

R.S. Daniell

Adult

This small warbler has a *short tail which it often holds up in a cocked position*. The head, mantle, rump and underparts are grey, and contrast with the *bright green wings*. The *eyes are red*. A widespread bird, it occurs singly or in pairs in woodland and thornbush country up to 2 000 m. Although fairly common, it is often difficult to see as it tends to skulk low down in dense bushes. The bird's call, a bleating 'quee queee', is often the first sign of its presence in an area; it also utters a sound which resembles the sound of two stones being knocked together.

Rattling Cisticola *Cisticola chiniana* **KTU 13 cm**

Adult

D. Richards

Often first recognised by its distinctive rattling 'che che che cheee' call, this cisticola has *a rufous-brown crown with indistinct streaking*. The mantle is similar *but is thickly streaked*, the tail is brown with pale tips, and the underparts are paler. It has a short, strong bill. Sexes are similar, but female is smaller than male. Immature is less streaked than adult and is yellowish below. Common, found in pairs or small groups in dry thornbush and scrub. Typically calls from bush tops.

Hunter's Cisticola *Cisticola hunteri* **KTU 14 cm**

A plain-looking cisticola, the top of the head is *rufous-brown merging to brown on the mantle and back*. The back is indistinctly streaked. It is grey below, but paler on the throat. Sexes are similar, and immature resembles adult but is duller. *Common in the highlands*, along forest edges and glades, and on moorland. Its loud, far-carrying call, a rhythmic, undulating trill, is given by two or more birds from the top of a bush or grass stem. The similar Chubb's Cisticola, *C. chubby*, (not illustrated) also duets but occurs in thick bush and forest edges in the west of the region.

Adult

D. Richards

99

Tawny-flanked Prinia *Prinia subflava* KTU 13 cm

This small, slim, long tailed warbler is brown in colour and has a *conspicuous pale super-cilium.* Sexes are similar, and immature resembles the adult but is duller and has a shorter tail. Usually found in pairs or in family groups, and is common, oc-curring in rank grass, scrub and along forest edges. Commonly draws attention to itself by way of its per-sistent 'prezztt … prezztt' call, *frequently raising and lowering its tail* at the same time. The Pale Prinia, *P. somalica,* (not illustrated) is similar, also showing a pale supercilium, but is grey above and whitish below; also, that species occurs in semi-arid country in north and north-east Kenya.

Adult

D. Richards

Red-faced Crombec *Sylvietta whytii* KTU 10 cm

A plump, *almost tailless* warbler, grey above and rufous below, becoming paler on the lower belly. The *sides of the face are rufous.* Sexes are similar, and immature is brownish grey. Occurs in pairs in acacia bush and along forest edges, and is usually seen climbing among branches of trees and bushes in search of small insects. Utters a brief warbling song, and also a 'tie tie' call note. The similar Northern Crombec, *S. brachyuran,* (not il-lustrated) is smaller and has a pale eye-stripe. Both species build a deep pouch-shaped nest of webs, grass heads and bark.

Adult

P.J. Ginn

African Grey Flycatcher *Bradornis microrhynchus* KTU 13 cm

Adult

D. Richards

An *all-grey flycatcher*, paler below and with *indistinct streaking on the crown* which is often difficult to see. Sexes are similar, and juveniles are distinctly spotted; immature is brownish. Found singly or in pairs in dry bush and acacia woodlands. The very similar Pale Flycatcher, *B. pallidus,* (not illustrated) is pale brown, longer-tailed, and occurs in less arid habitat. The Ashy Flycatcher, *Muscicapa carulescens,* (not illustrated) is paler grey with white streaks above and below the eyes.

Silverbird *Empidornis semipartitus* KTU 18 cm

Adult

R.S. Daniell

An unmistakable bird. The *upperparts are silvery grey,* and the *underparts* are *rufous in colour*. Sexes are alike, and immature is buffy above and spotted below. Locally common but generally uncommon. Usually found in pairs in dry bush and acacia woodlands where they sit in the open on the tops of bushes or telephone wires. They hawk for insects in the air but may also capture insect prey on the ground. The call is a sweet, thrush-like song.

White-eyed Slaty Flycatcher *Melaenornis fischeri* KTU **15 cm**

A stocky flycatcher with a distinctive *white ring around the eyes.* The upperparts are slate grey, and the underparts are paler. Sexes are alike, and immature is greyish brown, heavily spotted with white. A common highland bird, it is found singly or in pairs along forest edges and scrub. Common in garden in the highlands. Feeds mostly by picking up insects from the ground but also occasionally hawks them. Sometimes feeds on small ripe berries. At times, it may be seen feeding on the ground along forest and woodland tracks. Very active at dawn and dusk when it is also most vocal, uttering a sharp 'zit'.

D. Richards

Adult

Northern Black Flycatcher *Melaenornis edolioides* KTU **19 cm**

This dull black fly-catcher has a long, slender, square tail and diagnostic dark brown eyes. Sexes are alike, and immature is slaty black with chestnut spotting. Found singly or in pairs, in woodland and cultivated areas. *Catches its insect prey on the ground.* The Southern Black Fly-catcher, *M. pammelaina*, (not illustrated) is very similar but has glossy-black plumage and occurs in more arid areas. Both species are distinguished from adult Drongo (p. 89) by having a square (not forked) tail, dark (not red) eyes and a smaller, more slender bill.

D. Richards

Adult

African Dusky Flycatcher *Muscicapa adusta* KTU **10 cm**

This small, plump, short-tailed flycatcher is mainly brown-grey in colour although *paler on the throat and belly*. Sexes are alike, and immature is spotted buff above, and buffy below with brown spots. A tame bird, usually seen sitting on a bare branch from which it makes short flights. Common in the highlands where it occurs along forest edges, in woodland and in cultivated areas. The Spotted Flycatcher, *M. striata,* (not illustrated) is also brownish but has streaks down the front and is larger and longer-tailed. Similarly, the Swamp Flycatcher, *M. aquatica,* (not illustrated) is brown but larger and has a distinctive white throat and belly.

Adult

D. Richards

Chin-spot Batis *Batis molitor* KTU **10 cm**

N. Myburgh

Male

Female

N. Myburgh

A small, dumpy, short-tailed flycatcher. Male is grey above with black wings, a black tail and a black face. The underparts are white with a broad black band across the chest. Female is similar to male but has a rufous chest band and a small rufous spot on the throat. Immature is similar to female but duller, and is streaked on the upperparts and throat. Gives a distinctive, thin, flute-like song of three descending notes which has been interpreted as 'three blind mice', uttered repeatedly. Usually found in pairs or small family parties along forest edges or in acacia woodland.

103

African Paradise-Flycatcher *Terpsiphone viridis* KTU m – 30 – 36 cm, f = 20 cm

Male

D. Richards

Male (white phase)

D. Richards

A distinctive and unmistakable bird, the male has a *blackish-blue head with a bright blue bill and eye-ring; the back and tail are chestnut and the under-parts are grey*. Female is similar, but has a shorter tail and a duller blue eye-ring and bill. Immature resembles female. A white colour phase occurs: some males, particularly in eastern areas, have a white back and tail (females do not show this variation). Widespread and common, along forest edges, in woodlands and gardens.

Plain-backed Pipit *Anthus leucophrys* KTU 17 cm

D. Richards

Adult

A large, robust long-legged pipit, with uniformly dark brown upperparts, paler underparts with indistinct darker streaking on the breast, and buffy outer tail feathers. There is a pale eye-stripe above the eye and blackish moustachial stripes. The base of the lower mandible is yellowish. Sexes are similar, and immature resembles adult but has darker marks on the back. Found singly or in pairs, feeding on the ground in savannahs, grassland and in other short-grass areas. The similar Buffy Pipit, *A. vaalensis*, (not illustrated) is a rare visitor to southern Tanzania.

African (Grassland) Pipit *Anthus cinnamomeus* KTU 15 cm

Smaller and slimmer than the Plain-backed Pipit, this species also has *richer brown upperparts with darker streaking.* The white eye-stripe and *white outer tail feathers* are diagnostic. Below it is buffy with dark brown streaks on the chest forming a necklace. Sexes are similar, and immature resembles adult but is darker and more heavily streaked above. Widespread and common, this pipit occurs in almost any open grassland. The Long-billed Pipit. *A. similis,* (not illustrated) is similar to this

Adult

species but is larger, longer tailed and is less boldly marked on the face and back; also, the outer tail feathers are buffy, not white, in colour.

D. Richards

Rosy-breasted Longclaw *Macronyx ameliae* KTU 19 cm

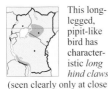

This long-legged, pipit-like bird has characteristic *long hind claws* (seen clearly only at close quarters). The upperparts are brown with black streaking, and the underparts are bright *salmon-pink with a broad black band across the chest. The outer tail feathers are white.* Female is duller than male and lacks the black chest band; immature shows no pink colouring below and also lacks the chest band. Utters a plaintive call, frequently given when fluttering low over grassland, at which time its legs are often lowered. Found in open grassland and swampy areas.

Male

D. Richards

105

Yellow-throated Longclaw *Macronyx croceus* KTU **20 cm**

Adult

The *bright yellow underparts* and throat encircled by a black band are distinctive. Above it is brown with darker streaking. Sexes are similar but female is duller than male. Immature is paler than adult. Usually seen fluttering low over grasslands when its white-tipped outer tail feathers are conspicuous. Its song, uttered mostly from the top of a bush but sometimes in flight, is a drawn-out 'twe whee', and is a characteristic sound of the open grasslands. The Pangani Longclaw, *M. aurantiigula*, (not illustrated) is similar but has an orange-yellow throat encircled by a less distinct band and the yellow coloration below is confined to the belly.

African Pied Wagtail *Motacilla aguimp* KTU **20 cm**

Adult

A distinctive *black and white bird with a long tail.* Sexes are similar, and immature is shorter-tailed and brownish where the adult is black. Common and widespread, it is confiding and is associated with human habitation. The Cape Wagtail, *M. capensis,* (not illustrated) is smaller, has grey upperparts, a thin greyish line over the eye, and less white on the wings. The Mountain Wagtail, *M. clara,* (not illustrated) differs from both by having a longer tail and a blue-grey back; also, it is always associated with fast-flowing streams and waterfalls.

D. Richards

Tropical Boubou *Laniarius aethiopicus* **KTU 23 cm**

Adult

This stout-looking black and white bird has a white wing bar, a pinkish wash on the belly, and a strong, hook-tipped bill. Sexes are similar, and immature is brownish. Common and widespread, it is found singly or in pairs but because of its skulking nature is often difficult to see. Found in forests, dense thickets, gardens and coastal scrub. Its well-known, bell-like call, 'bou bou bou', closely followed by a harsh 'kwee', is given in duet. The similar Common Fiscal (p. 109) is more conspicuous, slimmer, and has a long tail. The Black-backed Puffback, *Dryoscopus cubla*, (not illustrated) is also similar but is a tree-top species with a greyish-white rump.

Slate-coloured Boubou *Laniarius funebris* **KTU 18 cm**

Adult

A dark slaty-black bird with red eyes. Sexes are similar, and immature is brownish with indistinct barring above. A *skulking bird* which can be difficult to see, it is perhaps best known for its distinctive call – a bell-like 'bop bop' uttered by the male and closely answered by the female's higher 'boop'. Common and widespread, it usually occurs in more arid areas than Tropical Boubou, inhabiting dense thickets and coastal scrub usually below 1 500 m. Its skulking habit distinguishes it from Fork-tailed Drongo (p. 89) and Northern Black Flycatcher (p. 102)

107

Rosy-patched Bush-Shrike *Rhodophoneus cruentus* KT 23 cm

This slim, long-tailed shrike has buffy-brown upperparts and a rosy-red rump, conspicuous in flight. The tail is darker and there are white tips to the outer tail feathers. Below it is white with distinctive *rosy-red colouring on the throat and breast*. Female is similar to male but has a white throat surrounded by a black gorget and a rosy patch down the centre of the belly. Immature resembles adult but is duller. This shrike spends most of its time on the ground, but sings from the top of a bush: a thin melodious whistle consisting of several notes, 'deek dee dee'. Occurs in pairs in dry, open bush country usually below 1 300 m.

D. Richards

Adult

Long-tailed Fiscal *Lanius cabanisi* KT 30 cm

The upperparts of this shrike are black with a *grey rump and lower back* and an entirely black tail; *a small white bar is visible in the folded wing*. The underparts are white. Sexes are similar, and immature is brown with fine, darker barring. A conspicuous bird, it occurs in small parties which often perch in a bush swinging their tails up, down and around. Found in open woodlands and in grasslands with scattered bushes. The larger Magpie Shrike, *Corvinella melanoleuca*, (not illustrated) is all black with white patches on the sides of the mantle, and a grey rump.

D. Richards

Adult

108

Common Fiscal *Lanius collaris* **KTU 23 cm**

Smaller than the Long-tailed Fiscal, this bird has conspicuous *white marks on the wings and a grey rump. The tail is black above with white tips*, and white below. Sexes are similar, and immature is brown with fine barring. A widespread and common bird in open country, especially in the highlands. Conspicuous, perching in the open, often on telephone poles, it also frequents villages, towns and gardens. The Grey-backed Fiscal, *L. excubitorius*, (not illustrated) has grey upperparts and a white tail with black tips. The uncommon Mackinnon's Fiscal, *L. mackinnoni* (not illustrated) has grey upperparts and a conspicuous white stripe over the eye.

Adult

D. Richards

Taita Fiscal *Lanius dorsalis* **KTU 20 cm**

Adult

D. Richards

Similar to the Common Fiscal but distinguished by its *grey-blue mantle*. Sexes are alike, and immature is brown above with fine barring, and whitish below. Usually conspicuous, it perches on the tops of acacia bushes or trees in dry bush country. The Somali Fiscal, *L. somalicus*, (not illustrated) is similar but differs by having the secondaries broadly tipped with white (very conspicuous in flight) and, further, it occurs only in the Lake Turkana area and in Marsabit.

109

Northern White-crowned Shrike *Eurocephalus rueppelli* **KTU 23 cm**

Adult

The *upperparts of this bird are mainly pale brown and it has a white crown and forehead.* There is a thin black line through each eye and a black patch behind the eye. The underparts are white becoming buffy on the lower belly and flanks. Sexes are similar, and immature is duller than adult and has a brown crown. The characteristic fluttering and gliding flight is performed with the wings held slightly upwards. Occurs in pairs or small family parties in acacia bush country.

Violet-backed Starling *Cinnyricinclus leucogaster* **KTU 16 cm**

The violet-blue (appearing purple in some lights) upperparts and throat and the bright yellow eyes are characteristic. The underparts are white. Female is conspicuously different from the male, with brown upperparts mottled tawny, and white underparts with brown streaks. Immature is similar to the female. Locally common, particularly when fig trees are in fruit when it occurs in noisy flocks in forests, woodlands, gardens and bush country with figs. The similar Sharpe's Starling, *C. Charpii,* (not illustrated), a forest species, has a black back and head.

Male

110

Golden-breasted Starling *Cosmopsarus regius* KT 30 – 36 cm

Adult

The most beautiful of the starlings with a striking golden-yellow breast and belly. The upperparts are violet-blue and it has a long, slim, graduated tail and distinctive white eyes. Sexes are similar, and immature is paler than the adults and has a short tail. A very shy starling, occurring in pairs or loose flocks in dry bush and thornbush country. The all-grey Ashy Starling, *C. unicolor*, (not illustrated) also has a long tail and similar habits to this species but occurs in southern Tanzania.

Wattled Starling *Creatophora cinerea* KTU 21 cm

Non-breeding male

Breeding male

A pale grey starling with black wings and tail and a white rump (conspicuous in flight). Breeding male is distinctive with black bare skin on the forehead, face and throat, black wattles, and a bright yellow area behind the dark eyes. Female lacks the black wattles and yellow face patch, and immature is similar to female but duller. Highly gregarious, it occurs at times in large flocks – characterised by a continuous din of squeaky whistles. Often occurs among herds of game. Found in savannahs, acacia woodlands and pastures. Fischer's Starling, *Spero fishceri*, (not illustrated) is also grey but has a white belly and white eyes.

Greater Blue-eared Starling *Lamprotornis chalybaeus* **KTU 23 cm**

D. Richards

Adult

The upperparts of this starling are glossy green-blue and there is a row of black spots on the wing coverts; the underparts are bluer, darkening on the belly. The eyes are striking yellow-orange, and the ear coverts are dark. Sexes are alike, and immature is black, not blue, below. Widespread and common in woodlands and open country, it occurs in small groups or large flocks. The very similar Lesser Blue-eared Starling, *L. chloropterus*, (not illustrated) is difficult to separate. It is smaller, slimmer, and immatures are dark brown below.

Rüppell's Long-tailed Starling *Lamprotornis purpuropterus* **KTU 33 – 36 cm**

D. Richards

Adult

An iridescent, *dark purple-blue starling, with a long, graduated tail and creamy-white eyes.* The head and neck are darker, sometimes with a bronzy sheen. Sexes are similar, and immature is brownish with a shorter tail. Mostly found in pairs or small groups in acacia woodland and savannah country. The Bristle-crowned Starling, *Onychognathus salvadorii*, (not illustrated) also has a long, graduated tail but has distinctive chestnut in the primaries and a conspicuous forehead tuft.

Hildebrandt's Starling *Lamprotornis hildebrandti* KT **18 cm**

Adult

The dark glossy-blue upperparts, *deep rufous breast and belly,* and the striking *dark orange-red eyes* distinguish this bird. Sexes are similar, and immature resembles adult but is duller. Gregarious in small groups, it feeds on the ground in savannah woodlands, acacia country and cultivation. Often confused with the Superb Starling, but can be distinguished by its lack of white underwings and white undertail coverts, and by its dark, not pale, eyes: also, lacks the white line separating the throat and belly as seen in that species.

Superb Starling *Lamprotornis superbus* KTU **18 cm**

Adult

East Africa's best-known starling, with iridescent blue-green upperparts and black spots on the wing. The head is blackish and the *eyes are pale yellow.* The *rich orange-chestnut belly is separated from the throat by a white line. The underwings and undertail coverts are white.* Sexes are similar, and immature is duller than adult and has dark eyes. Common and widespread, it is found in a wide variety of habitats. Similar to Hildebrandt's Starling (see above for differences).

Yellow-billed Oxpecker *Buphagus africanus* KTU 19 cm

Adult

Similar in appearance to the Red-billed Oxpecker but with a distinctive *red-tipped yellow bill and red eyes*. The upperparts are ashy-brown with a *pale buffy rump*, and the throat and upper chest are ashy-brown merging to buff on the belly. Sexes are similar, and *immature* is duller than adult and has a *pale rump*, dark eyes and a brown bill. Widespread throughout the region, and closely associated with game and cattle. Oxpeckers are specially adapted to feed on ticks and other insects found on mammals. Their claws are sharp and strong and their tail feathers are very stiff, similar to a woodpecker. This oxpecker utters a distinctive 'tseee, tseee' call.

Red-billed Oxpecker *Buphagus erythrorhynchus* KTU 18 cm

Adult

Similar to the Yellow-billed Oxpecker but with *bright red bill and red eyes surrounded by a yellow eye-ring*. The upperparts including the *rump* are *ashy-brown*, and the underparts are ashy-brown merging to buff on the belly. Sexes are similar, and immature is duller than adult with dark eyes and a black bill. Widespread, but more common than the Yellow-billed Oxpecker and also associated with game and cattle. Its call is similar to that of the Yellow-billed Oxpecker.

Eastern Violet-backed Sunbird *Anthreptes orientalis* KTU 11,5 cm

Female

Male

The male bird has violet-blue upperparts, a violet-blue throat and white underparts. The *female* is brown-grey above and has a distinctive *white eye-stripe*; the underparts are white and the uppertail coverts and tail are dark violet. Immature is similar to female. Locally common in semi-arid bush country, often near water. These birds are reputed to often build their nests close to wasp's nests. The similar Western Violet-backed Sunbird, *A. longuemarei*, (not illustrated) is a larger bird (13 cm), the male is grey below, and the female is yellowish below; also it is much less common and is a woodland species that occurs in the western parts of the region.

Amethyst Sunbird *Chalcomitra amethystina* KTU 12,5 cm

Male

A velvety-black-coloured sunbird with a long de-curved bill. At close range the *chin and throat are seen to be rosy purple* and the top of the head is metallic green. The female is brown with a pale eye-stripe, and is paler below with heavy streaking. Immature is similar to female. The male utters a pleasant warbling song. Widespread, this sunbird occurs in a wide variety of habitats, from forest edges to gardens up to 2 200 m altitudes.

115

Red-chested Sunbird *Cinnyris erythorcercus* KTU 13 – 15 cm

Male

The male is *metallic green on the head,* neck and mantle, and below shows a *deep-red chest band and a black belly; the elongated central tail feathers* are distinctive. In some lights a metallic-violet band can be seen across the chest, and also on the rump and uppertail coverts. Female is dark brown above and buffy below; the central tail feathers are less elongated than in male. Locally common between 600 m and 1 800 m, especially near water, and especially *common around the shores of Lake Victoria.*

Sometimes confused with Scarlet-chested Sunbird (p. 118) but the long tail, green head and black belly should avoid confusion.

Hunter's Sunbird *Chalcomitra hunteri* KTU 14 cm

Female

Male

Similar to and often confused with the Scarlet-chested Sunbird (p. 118). The *male is all black* with a metallic-green cap and green moustachial streaks. The *throat is all black* bordering on to a bright scarlet chest. In some lights the *violet rump and violet patches on the wing* can be seen. Female is brown, mottled and streaked below, and immature is similar to female. Widespread in bush country and woodland in semi-arid areas between 50 m and 1 500 m.

116

Bronze Sunbird *Nectarinia kilimensis* KTU 14 – 23 cm

Female

A blackish-looking, long-tailed sunbird with a *metallic bronze-green head, throat,* *Male*

shoulders and chest, which in some lights appear green. Female is paler than male, olive-grey above and yellowish below with darker streaking, and has a shorter tail. Immature is similar to female. A highland species, locally common, and occurring along forest edges, in cultivated land and in gardens. Sometimes confused with the Malachite Sunbird, *N. famosa*, (not illustrated) but male Malachite is an unmistakable bright emerald green: female is unstreaked below.

Marico Sunbird *Cinnyris mariquensis* KTU 13 cm

Male   *Female*

The metallic-green upperparts and throat show a coppery sheen – seen only in some lights. *A thin blue line separates the throat from a broad maroon chest band; the belly is black*. Female is grey-brown above with a buffy eye-stripe and is paler below with dusky streaks. Immature is similar to female but has a dark throat. Occurs in savannah and acacia scrub, and in woodland. The similar Purple-banded Sunbird, *C. bifusciata*, (not illustrated) has a broader maroon chest band.

Beautiful Sunbird *Cinnyris pulchella* KTU 12 – 15 cm

Male

D. Richards

A small, slender-looking sunbird with a long thin tail, bright metallic-green upperparts and a *red chest with yellow sides*. The belly colour is variable according to region: east of the Rift Valley it is black while west of it, it is green – apart from an area around Kisumu in western Kenya where males show a black belly. Female has a short tail, is all grey with pale eye-stripes, and below shows indistinct streaking. Immature is similar to female. Occurs in acacia woodland and savannahs. The very similar Black-bellied Sunbird, *C. nectarinoides*, (not illustrated) is smaller, lacks the yellow chest patches and always shows a black belly.

Scarlet-chested Sunbird *Chalcomitra senegalensis* KTU 15 cm

R.S. Daniell

Male

ABPL / B. Ryan

Female

This *velvety brown or blackish sunbird* has a metallic-green cap and moustachial streaks; *throat is also metallic green* but is often difficult to see. The *vivid scarlet chest is spotted bright metallic blue* (seen in some lights only). Female is dark brown above, and buffy below with mottling and streaking. Immature is similar to female but has blackish streaks below. Occurs in various habitats, preferring medium- to high-rainfall areas. May be confused with Hunter's Sunbird (p. 116), and with Red-chested Sunbird (p. 116) which is distinguished by its long tail and black belly.

Variable Sunbird *Cinnyris venustus* **KTU 9 cm**

Female

Male

The male bird is a *metallic blue-green above with dark wings and a dark tail. The throat and the upper chest are bright metallic purple-violet* and the remaining underparts are bright yellow. Female is olive-grey above, and below is whitish and unstreaked. Immature resembles female. Widespread, this sunbird occurs along forest edges, in woodland and in gardens. The similar Collared Sunbird, *Hedydipna collaris*, (not illustrated) has a green head and neck, lacks the purple-violet chest band and has a much shorter bill.

D. Richards

Yellow White-eye *Zosterops senegalensis* **KTU 10 cm**

A bright *yellowish-green bird with a fine, pointed bill, a narrow white eye-ring, and a distinctive yellow forehead* which contrasts with the rest of the head. Sexes are similar, and immature resembles adult but is duller. Occurs in pairs or small groups along forest edges and in woodland, west of the Rift Valley. The very similar Abyssinian White-eye, *A. abyssinica* (not illustrated) has the whole of the head yellow, and occurs both in and east of the Rift Valley. The Montane or Kikuyu White-eye, *Z. poligastra*, (not illustrated) is larger and greener, and occurs in the highlands.

Adult

P. Davey

119

Grosbeak Weaver (Thick-billed Weaver) *Amblyospiza albifrons* KTU 18 cm

Female

This large thickset weaver has a distinctive, *large heavy bill*. Male is slate-black or brownish-black with a *white patch on the forehead* and a small white wing patch, conspicuous in flight. Female is brown above and paler below with dark streaks, has a paler bill, and a yellowish lower mandible. Immature is similar to female but has a yellower bill and a yellow gape. Usually occurs in small groups near water, and nests in reedbeds. Builds a distinctive neat and compact nest of fine shredded leaves or reeds. The similar Thick-billed Seedeater, *Serinus burtoni*, (not illustrated), a shy highland forest species, is dark brown with faint dark streaking, has a small white patch on the forehead, and shows green-edged wings and tail.

Male

Red-headed Weaver *Anaplectes rubriceps* KTU 15 cm

Male *Female*

The male is easily identified by its *bright crimson-red crown, nape, throat and chest* and by its black face and red bill. The back, wings and tail are brown and the belly is white. Female is greyish with *conspicuous red edges to the flight and tail feathers*, a pale pink bill, and pale underparts. Non-breeding male resembles female but has an orange-yellow bill, and immature resembles female but has a pale brown bill. Widely distributed, it occurs in woodland and acacia bush.

R.S. Daniell

D. Richards

P.J. Ginn

120

Red-collared Widowbird *Euplectes ardens* KTU m = 28 cm; f = 13 cm

Breeding male is *all black and has a red, crescent-shaped patch across the chest, and a long tail.* Birds in the Kenya highlands have the red on the chest extending on to the nape and crown. Non-breeding male is dusky-brown above with heavy streaking, buffy below, and has blackish wings. Female and immature resemble non-breeding male but have less distinct streaking above. Male is conspicuous during the breeding season, when it flutters from bush to bush in display, its long, flowing tail hanging down. Widespread and locally common, it is found in grasslands, open bush country and also in cultivated land.

D. Richards

Breeding male

Yellow Bishop *Euplectes capensis* KTU 15 cm

R.S. Daniell

P.J. Ginn

Breeding male   *Female*

Breeding male is black with a conspicuous bright yellow rump and yellow shoulder patches. Non-breeding male is brown, heavily streaked, with blackish wings and a blackish tail, and retains the yellow rump and shoulders. Female and immature are similar to non-breeding male, but not as heavily streaked, have brown wings and tail, a paler yellow rump and lack the yellow shoulders. Widespread and common in the highlands along forest edges and in grasslands.

121

Yellow-mantled Widowbird *Euplectes macrourus* **KTU m = 31 cm; f = 11 cm**

Male

Female

P.J. Ginn

P.J. Ginn

Breeding male is all black, but differs from Yellow Bishop (p. 121) by its long tail and *bright yellow mantle and shoulders* (not rump). Non-breeding male is brown, heavily streaked, with blackish wings and tail; retains yellow shoulders but loses the long tail. Males in Uganda and western Kenya lack the yellow mantle but show yellow shoulders. Female and immature resemble non-breeding male but are paler and lack the yellow shoulders. Locally common in grasslands, marshes and along edges of lakes and swamps. Gregarious when not breeding.

Long-tailed Widowbird *Euplectes progne* **K m = 61 – 76 cm; f = 15 cm**

D. Richards

Breeding male

HPH Photography / Photo Access

Female

The male in breeding dress is *all black with an extremely long, floppy tail* and red shoulder patches. Non-breeding male is tawny-buff, heavily streaked above, and retains the red shoulder patches but loses the long tail. Female and immature resemble the non-breeding male but lack the red shoulder patches. Locally common and conspicuous in the Kenya highlands, in grassland and in moorland. The male displays by flying low over its area with very *slow heavy wing-beats and with the tail conspicuously drooped*. Very gregarious in the non-breeding season. Builds a domed nest of grass close to the ground.

Baglafecht Weaver *Ploceus baglafecht* **KTU 15 cm**

Female

Male

D. Richards

D. Richards

The male is *yellow with a black nape, back, tail and ear coverts, and has pale eyes. Female* is similar to male but has a *black head*. Immature resembles female but is duller. A *non-colonial* species, widespread and common mainly in the highlands along forest edges, woodlands and in gardens. The similar Black-necked Weaver, *P. nigricollis*, (not illustrated) is more golden yellow, the male has a black chin and throat and a thin black line through the eyes. Female has a black cap and neck and a black line through the eyes. Occurs at lower altitudes.

Taveta Golden Weaver *Ploceus castaneiceps* **KT 14 cm**

Male

Female

D. Richards

Bruce Coleman / G. Cubitt

A bright yellow weaver with a *golden-chestnut patch on the head and golden-chestnut wash on the chest*. The wings and tail are greenish, and the eyes are black. Female is dull yellow with dusky streaking, and immature is similar to female. Locally common in riverine vegetation and along rivers and swamps. *Breeds colonially* over water. The similar Golden Palm Weaver, *P. bojeri*, (not illustrated) has the whole of the head bright orange, brown eyes, and breeds mostly in trees, particularly in palms and bushes. The Northern Golden Weaver, *P. subaureus*, (not illustrated) is also similar but is bright yellow with a golden wash over the head, and has pale red eyes.

123

Black-headed Weaver (Village Weaver) *Ploceus cucullatus* KTU 17 – 18 cm

Male

A bright yellow weaver with a black head, black flight feathers and tail, and red eyes. Two distinct races occur. The eastern race has the mantle spotted, and the western race has the mantle yellow-orange. Female and immature are olive-brown above with dusky streaks, yellowish below, and have *red eyes. Highly gregarious, these birds breed in colonies, often near human habitation.* Widespread and common in open country with scattered trees, in woodlands and in gardens. Outside of the breeding season the birds often form large flocks which frequent grasslands.

Female

Spectacled Weaver *Plocues ocularis* KTU 15 cm

Male

A bright yellow bird with greenish wings and tail. Male has a black bib on the chin and throat, and a black patch through the eyes. Female is similar to male but the bib on the chin and throat is orange, not black. Immature resembles female but is duller. The call is distinctive, a descending 'tee…tee…tee'. Locally common, but shy and more skulking than other weavers, it occurs in forests and acacia woodland, particularly along rivers and streams and is not colonial.

Female

124

Speke's Weaver *Ploceus spekei* **KT 15 cm**

D. Richards

P. Davey

Male   *Female*

Male has a *yellow back with distinctive black markings*, pale eyes and a yellow forehead, crown and nape. The sides of the face, chin and throat are black. Female and immature are olive-brown above with darker mottling, and buffy-white below. Found in the highlands in various habitats, and breeds in colonies, often near human habitation. The Lesser Masked Weaver, *P. intermedius*, (not illustrated) is similar but has yellow eyes, a black crown, face, chin and throat, and a greenish-yellow back.

Holub's Golden Weaver *Ploceus xanthops* **KTU 18 cm**

A large thickset, bright yellow weaver with a *large, heavy, black bill and pale eyes.* Male has an orange wash on the throat and chest, and female is paler overall and lacks the orange wash. Immature resembles female but is duller. Widespread, and not a gregarious bird, it occurs singly or in pairs in a variety of habitats, from dense vegetation to cultivated land. The Orange Weaver, *P. aurantius*, (not illustrated) also has pale eyes, but is smaller (13 cm), has a pale bill, and the head is orange-yellow; it occurs mainly around the shores of Lake Victoria.

Male

Female

D. Richards

D. Richards

125

Red-billed Quelea *Quelea quelea* KTU 13 cm

Breeding male

Breeding male has a distinctive *black face and a red bill*; the upperparts are brown and heavily streaked, and there is a pinkish wash around the head, shoulders and chest; the underparts are buffy. Non-breeding male lacks the black face but retains the red bill. Female and immature resemble non-breeding male but have a pale bill and a pale eye-stripe. Widespread, common and very gregarious, occurring in dry thornbush and cultivated country. The Red-headed Quelea, *Q. erythrops*, (not illustrated) is similar but has a red head when breeding, a dark bill, a streaked back but streaking on the neck; female is difficult to separate from other queleas.

Red-billed Buffalo-Weaver *Bubalornis niger* KT 26 cm

Female

A large stout *all-black weaver with white-edged flight feathers and a large red bill*. Female has a blackish bill and is grey-brown above with streaks, and paler below with streaks. Immature is similar to female but has white edgings to the feathers. Common and gregarious, it occurs in savannah and acacia woodland, and nests colonially. Its *large stick nest is distinctive and most often built in baobab trees*. Male White-billed Buffalo-Weaver, *B. albi-rostris*, (not illustrated) is similar but has a white bill, and occurs in western Kenya and Uganda.

Male

126

White-headed Buffalo-Weaver *Dinemellia dinemelli* **KTU 23 cm**

Adult

An unmistakable, large, stocky weaver, with a *white head, chest and belly* and a brown mantle, wings and tail. The *rump and both the upper and lower tail coverts are orange-red* (especially conspicuous in flight). Sexes are similar, and immature resembles adult but is duller and browner. Widespread, occurring in pairs or small groups and usually seen feeding on the ground in dry bush and acacia woodland below 1 400 m. Breeds in loose colonies, building an untidy domed nest.

Rufous-tailed Weaver *Histurgops ruficauda* **KT 22 cm**

Adult

A very conspicuous and noisy weaver. The upperparts are brown with pale edging to the feathers, which imparts a distinctive mottled effect, and the underparts are paler with brown mottling. In flight the brown tail, chestnut outer tail feathers and chestnut edges to the flight feathers are conspicuous. The eyes are pale blue. Sexes are similar, and immature resembles adult but is browner. A locally very common bird, occurring in noisy flocks, and feeding on the ground in dry acacia woodland and grasslands with scattered trees.

127

White-browed Sparrow-Weaver *Plocepasser mahali* KTU 15 cm

A mainly brown weaver with a *conspicuous broad white eye-stripe,* white wing coverts and a *white rump* – particularly noticeable in flight. The underparts are white. Sexes are similar, and immature resembles adult but is duller. A very common bird, occurring in noisy flocks in dry acacia and savannah country, and the untidy round grass nests it builds are a feature of the landscape. The nests have two entrances and are used all year round as roosting sites, but when breeding commences one of the entrances is sealed off by the female and the inside of the nest is lined with fine grasses.

Adult

D. Richards

Grey-capped Social Weaver *Pseudonigrita arnaudi* KTU 13 cm

A *small, short-tailed greyish-buff bird with a dove-grey cap.* The eyes are deep red in colour and surrounded by a white eye-ring. Sexes are similar, and immature is buffy with the top of the head buffy-grey. Locally common in dry thorn and acacia country where it is gregarious, breeding in small scattered colonies, mostly below 1 400 m. The birds generally stay in the vicinity of these colonies all year round. The similar Black-capped Social Weaver, *P. cabanisi,* (not illustrated) can be distinguished by its black head, brown back and white underparts.

Adult

D. Richards

Chestnut Sparrow *Passer eminibey* **KTU 11 cm**

Breeding male

Breeding male is *rich chestnut* with a darker head and *dark eyes*. The wings and tail feathers are blackish with white edging. Non-breeding male and female have an ashy-brown head and neck, a black-streaked mantle, and a chocolate-brown eye-stripe, rump and shoulders. Immature resembles female. Gregarious, these birds occur in dry acacia bush country. The similar Chestnut Weaver, *Ploceus rubiginosus*, (not illustrated) is much larger; breeding male is chestnut-brown with a black head and red eyes; non-breeding male is ashy-brown above with a blackish-streaked head and mantle, and pale below.

Grey-headed Sparrow *Passer griseus* **KTY 15 – 18 cm**

A typical sparrow with a *grey head and neck, grey underparts,* a rufous-brown back, and with a *rufous rump and undertail coverts.* A number of races occur; the smallest of these has a buffy chin and throat and a small white mark on the shoulder; the largest has a large and distinctive parrot-like bill. Sexes are similar, and immature resembles the adult but is duller. These birds are widespread and common in a variety of habitats, including towns and villages. They build untidy nests, usually in a low tree or bush but occasionally in a tree hole or in another bird's nest.

Adult

129

Rufous Sparrow *Passer rufocinctus* **KTU 14 cm**

Female

Male

A typical sparrow, it has a grey mantle and crown, a *rich brown back with black streaking, and a rufous rump*. A distinctive rufous streak runs from the eyes to the nape and a black streak runs through each eye above the white cheeks. The male shows a black bib on the chin and throat, and the female a grey bib. Immature is similar to female. Found in a variety of habitats, including wooded grasslands, cultivated lands and gardens. The male House Sparrow, *P. domesticus*, (not illustrated) is similar but has a grey, not rufous, rump. The House Sparrow is slowly spreading through Kenya and Tanzania and has now reached Nairobi and Arusha, and is a threat to resident sparrows.

Yellow-spotted Petronia *Petronia pyrgita* **KTU 15 cm**

Adult

A very plain-looking, sparrow-like bird, brownish-grey with a buffy eye-stripe and a *pale eye-ring*. The underparts are greyish-white with an often *indistinct yellow mark on the throat*. Sexes are similar; immature resembles adult but lacks the yellow throat mark. Found in dry open acacia bush and savannah, where it has a preference for rocky ground. The very similar Yellow-throated Petronia, *P. superciliaris*, (not illustrated) occurs in central and southern Tanzania.

130

Village Indigobird *Vidua chalybeata* KTU 11 cm

Male

D. Richards

Breeding male is distinctive, all glossy blue-black above with a white bill and bright orange-red legs. A race occurring along the East African coast differs by having a red bill. Female and non-breeding male are similar with dark-streaked brown upperparts, a broad buff stripe down the centre of the crown and a buffy streak over the eye. The underparts are whitish, and the bill is horn-coloured. Immature is similar to female. A widespread species, found in open woodlands, cultivated lands and in gardens. In parasitises

Female

P.J. Ginn

the Red-billed Firefinch (p. 133). The male Variable Indigobird, *H. funereal*, (not illustrated) also shows a white bill when breeding but has whitish-pink legs.

Straw-tailed Whydah *Vidua fisheri* KTU m = 28 cm; f = 10 cm

The male in breeding plumage is unmistakable with a *creamy-coloured crown, breast and belly*; the remaining upperparts including the tail are black, and the bill is bright red. The *straw-coloured central tail feather is long and thin*. Non-breeding male is buff-coloured streaked with black, and has a short blackish tail but retains the red bill. Female is similar to non-breeding male, and immature resembles female but is duller. Usually found in small groups in dry bush and scrub country where it is widespread but not very common. Parasitises the Purple Grenadier (p. 135).

Breeding male

D. Richards

131

Pin-tailed Whydah *Vidua macroura* KTU m = 30 – 33 cm; f = 12 cm

Female

Breeding male
is unmistakable
with its *black and
white plumage,
long thin tail and
red bill*. Non-
breeding male,

Breeding male

female and immature have brown upperparts with darker streaking,
a buffy crown bordered by two black streaks, and are buffy below.
Breeding male has a very distinctive jerky display flight. Occurs in
grasslands, cultivated lands and in gardens. Parasitises waxbills.

Eastern Paradise-Whydah *Vidua paradisaea* KTU m = 38 – 41 cm; f = 13 cm

Breeding male
is unmistak-
able with a
long, distinc-
tively shaped,
*tapering, black
tail*. The head

Breeding male

and back are black separated
by a golden-buff collar, and the
underparts are buffy with a
rich chestnut breast. Female, non-
breeding male, and immature are
buffy above with dark streaks,
striped black and white on top of
the head, and buffy-white below.
Mostly found in dry acacia bush
and grasslands. The Broadtailed
Paradise-Whydah, *V. obtuse*,
(not illustrated) has a broader tail
which does not taper to a tip.

Female

132

Common Waxbill *Estrilda astrild* KTU **10 cm**

Adult

A small brown bird with a conspicuous *red bill and a red streak through the eyes*. The upperparts are dark brown with very fine barring, and the underparts are paler with fine dusky barring and a reddish patch in the centre of belly. Sexes are similar, and immature is duller than adult and has a brown bill. Occurs in flocks, in lush grasslands and overgrown cultivation, often near water. The similar Crimson-rumped Waxbill, *E. rhodopyga*, (not illustrated) has a crimson rump, crimson on the wings and is darker below.

Red-billed Firefinch *Lagonosticta senegala* KTU **9 cm**

Male (left) *and female* (right)

The male is pinkish red overall with small white dots on the chest, brown wings and tail, and a *greyish-red bill*. The eyes are red surrounded by a thin yellow eye-ring. Female and immature are duller than male, with dark eyes surrounded by a pale eye-ring. Found in pairs or family groups in grasslands and in gardens. The similar African Firefinch, *L. rubricata*, (not illustrated) is larger and redder overall and has a blue-black bill and black undertail coverts.

133

Green-winged Pytilia *Pytilia melba* KTU 13 cm

P.J. Ginn

Male

P.J. Ginn

Female

A distinctive bird with a *red face, a bright red bill and a crimson rump and tail*. The back of the head is grey, the wings and back are green, and the underparts are grey with *distinct dark barring*. Female and immature resemble male but lack the red face. Widespread but shy, the bird quickly takes to cover if disturbed. Occurs in pairs or in family groups in dry bush, acacia bush and neglected cultivation. The male Orange-winged Pytilia, *P. afra*, (not illustrated) is similar but has more red on the face, red edges to the wing feathers and fine barring below.

Red-cheeked Cordon-bleu *Uraeginthus bengalus* KTU 13 cm

D. Richards

Male

D. Richards

Female

A striking azure-blue and brown waxbill with a longish tail. Male has a *bright red patch on the cheeks and a dark red bill*. Female and immature are slightly duller than male and lack the red cheek patch. Widespread and common, the bird is found in pairs or family groups in thornbush and acacia grasslands, along forest edges and in gardens. The male Southern Cordon-bleu, *U. angolensis*, (not illustrated) is similar but lacks the red cheeks. The Blue-capped Cordon-bleu, *U. cyanocephalus*, (not illustrated) also lacks the red cheeks, and the male's head is entirely blue; also, found in more arid country than the other two species.

Purple Grenadier *Uraeginthus ianthinogaster* **KTU 14 cm**

Male

A distinctive-looking waxbill. The male's head, neck and throat are cinnamon merging to brown on the back and wings. The eyes are dark with red eyelids and are surrounded by a blue patch, and the bill is red. The rump and up-pertail coverts are cobalt-blue, and the underparts are cobalt-blue with cinnamon splashes. Female has a much reduced blue eye-patch and whitish eyelids; the underparts are russet-brown with small whitish spots. Immature resembles female but has no eye-patch and lacks the spotting below. A widespread and sometimes common bird, it occurs in dry country with thickets and scrub up to altitudes of 2 300 m. The Purple Grenadier is parasitised by the Straw-tailed Whydah (p. 131).

Immature

Female

135

Cut-throat Finch *Amadina fasciata* KTU 12 cm

Male (left) *and female* (right)

A small, speckled, brown bird with a large heavy bill. Male has a conspicuous red band around the throat and a rufous-brown belly. Female and immature are paler than male and lack the red throat band and rufous-brown belly. Locally common, it is found mostly in dry acacia bush country. When not breeding occurs in flocks, often in association with waxbills – particularly at waterholes. Although it builds its own nest, it often takes over those of other birds, such as Social Weavers.

African Citril *Serinus citrinelloides* KTU 11,5 cm

Female

Male

The male is yellow above with dark streaking, and has a *distinctive black face and throat* and a yellow eyestripe. The rump and belly are also yellow. Female lacks the black face of the male, and has a yellow throat with fine, blackish streaks. Immature is similar to female. Found in pairs or in small parties in open scrub country, neglected cultivation and in gardens, between altitudes of 1 100 m and 3 000 m. The male has a sweet whistling song.

136

African Golden-breasted Bunting *Emberiza flaviventris* **KTU 15 cm**

Adults

A small, long-tailed bird with a *conspicuous black and white striped head, a rich golden breast* and a yellow belly. The back is rufous-brown. It has white wing bars and white tips to the outer tail feathers. Usually found singly or in pairs in open woodland, savannahs and acacia bush. The similar Somali Golden-breasted Bunting, *E. poliopleura*, (not illustrated) can be separated by the mantle feathers which are edged white and by the white flanks; also, it occurs in more arid habitats.

Yellow-rumped Seed-eater *Serinus reichenowi* **KTU 10 cm**

Adult

This bird is brown above with dusky streaking, whitish below, and shows a pale eye-stripe. The *bright lemon-yellow rump* is diagnostic and is especially conspicuous in flight. Sexes are similar, and immature resembles adult but has a spotted breast. Occurs in pairs or in small flocks in open woodland, grasslands and in cultivated lands. The similar Streaky Seedeater, *S. striolatus*, (p. 139) is larger than this species and does not have a yellow rump.

Bronze Mannikin *Lonchura cucullata* **KTU 9 cm**

Adult

The *head, throat and upper chest are black with a bronzy wash*, the mantle and wings are ash-brown and the rump and tail coverts are barred black and white. The *white lower chest and belly* are distinctive, as are the *flanks which are barred black and white*. Sexes are similar, and immature is brown with a black tail. Tame and gregarious, these birds occur in savannah country, along forest edges and in gardens. The Black-and-White Mannikin, *L. bicolor,* (not illustrated) is similar and two distinct races occur; birds in the west have a black head, back, wings and tail and a white belly; eastern races are very distinctive and have conspicuous rufous back.

White-bellied Canary *Serinus dorsostriatus* **KTU 13 cm**

Adult

A typical canary with a *longish, forked tail*. The upperparts are greenish yellow with darker streaking, the throat and chest are yellow, and the *belly is white*. Female and immature are similar to the male but are generally duller. Widespread, these birds occur in small flocks in dry bush and grasslands, usually between 400 m and 1 400 m.

Yellow-fronted Canary *Serinus mozambicus* KTU 11,5 cm

Adult

The greenish-yellow upperparts have dusky streaking, and the forehead, throat, belly and *rump are bright yellow*. Face is yellow with dark moustachial stripes and there is a dusky streak through each eye. Sexes are similar, and immature resembles adult but is duller. Wide-ranging, this canary occurs in open woodlands, scrub, cultivation and in gardens. The Brimstone Canary, *S. sulphuratus*, (not illustrated) is larger, has a stouter bill, and the yellow rump does not contrast as sharply with upperparts. The Yellow-crowned Canary, *S. canicollis*, (not illustrated) is also similar but has a distinct yellow crown, darker markings on the back, conspicuous white wing bars, and is a highland bird.

Streaky Seed-eater *Serinus striolatus* KTU 15 cm

This bird has *brown upperparts with dark, heavy streaking and a con-spicuous white eye-stripe* which is diagnostic. The underparts are buffy and there is brown streaking on the throat, breast and flanks. Sexes are similar, and immature resembles adult but is duller. Occurs in pairs in the highlands, along forest edges, moorlands, scrub and also in gardens. The similar Streaky-headed Seed-eater, *S. gularis*, (not illustrated) is a scarce bird found in the west of the region, and is smaller, greyer above and whiter below.

Adult

Glossary of terms

Call Short notes given by male and female birds to indicate alarm or to contact other birds (*see* Song).

Cap The area encompassing the forehead and crown.

Casque A horny ridge on top of the bill (as seen in some species of hornbill).

Cere Coloured bare skin at the base of the upper mandible (as seen in raptors).

Colonial Associating in close proximity, either while roosting, feeding or nesting.

Crest Elongated feathers on the forehead, crown or nape.

Decurved Curving downward.

Display A pattern of behaviour in which a bird attracts attention while defending a territory or courting a female.

Eclipse Non-breeding or winter plumage.

Endemic Restricted to a certain region.

Eyebrow Usually referring to a stripe running above the eye.

Eye-ring A circle of coloured feathers around the eye.

Eye-stripe A stripe running from the base of the bill directly through the eye.

Feral Species that have escaped from captivity and now live in the wild.

Frontal shield A bare patch of skin, often brightly coloured, on the forehead.

Gorget A band of colour on the throat or upper breast.

Immature A bird that has moulted its juvenile plumage but has not yet attained its full adult plumage.

Juvenile The first full-feathered plumage of a young bird.

Migrant A species that undertakes long-distance flights between its wintering and breeding areas.

Moustachial stripes Lines running from the base of the bill to the sides of the throat.

Non-colonial A species that does not associate closely with other birds while roosting, feeding or nesting.

Nuptial plumage Breeding plumage.

Parasitize When a bird lays its eggs in the nest of another species for the purposes of incubation.

Plumage Feathering of a kind.

Polyandrous Having more than one male to each female.

Primaries The outermost major flight feathers of the wing.

Raptor A bird of prey.

Resident A bird that occurs throughout the year in a region and is not known to undertake migration.

Roost To sleep or rest, either in flocks or singly.

Ruff A natural growth of feathers seen around the necks of certain birds.

Rufous Reddish brown.

Secondaries Flight feathers of a bird's wing, adjoining the primary feathers.

Song A series of notes given by a male bird to proclaim its territory (*see* Call).

Speculum A patch of distinctive colour on the wing of a bird, usually best seen in flight.

Summer visitor A bird that is absent from the region during winter.

Territory An area that a bird establishes and subsequently defends from others.

Transitional adult A bird that is between breeding and non-breeding plumages and so shows characteristics of both.

Vent The area from the belly to the undertail coverts.

Parts of a bird

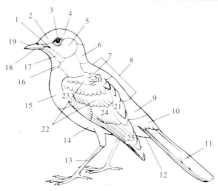

1 lores	10 uppertail coverts	17 malar region
2 forehead	11 tail	18 lower mandible
3 eye-ring	12 undertail coverts	19 upper mandible
4 crown	13 tarsus	20 scapulars
5 ear coverts	14 belly	21 tertials
6 nape	15 breast	22 wing coverts
7 mantle	16 throat	23 alula
8 back		24 secondaries
9 rump		25 primaries

Habitat map of East Africa

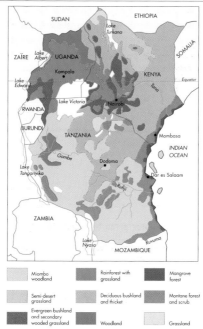

Miombo woodland

Semi-desert grassland

Evergreen bushland and secondary wooded grassland

Rainforest with grassland

Deciduous bushland and thicket

Woodland

Mangrove forest

Montane forest and scrub

Grassland

Further reading

Backhurst G.C. (ed). Scopus. 1977-1995. *Journal of the Ornithological Sub-committee of the East African Natural History Society.*

Bennun L., Gichuki C. & Fanshaw J. (eds). 1995-1995. *Kenya Birds* A joint publication of the Department of Ornithology, National Museums of Kenya and Birdlife Kenya.

Britton P.L. (ed). 1980. *Birds of East Africa: their habitats, status and distribution.* East African Natural History Society, Nairobi.

Brown, L.H., Urban, E.K., Newman, K.B., Fry, C.H. & Keith, S. (eds). 1982-84. *The Birds of Africa.* Vols 1-4, Academic Press, London.

Cambell, B. & Lack, E. 1985, *A Dictionary of Birds.* T & AD Poyser Calton.

Chandler, R.J. 1989. *North Atlantic Shorebirds.* Macmillan Press Ltd. London.

Guggisberg, C.A.W. 1980. *Birds of East Africa.* Vols 1 & 2. Mount Kenya Sundries Ltd, Nairobi.

Heinzel, H., Fitter, R. & Parslow, J. 1972. *The Birds of Britain and Europe with North Africa and the Middle East.* Collins, London.

Lewis, A. & Pomeroy, D. 1989. *A Bird Atlas of Kenya.* AA Balkema, Rotterdam.

Moore, R. 1982. *Where to Watch Birds in Kenya.* Transafrica Press, Nairobi.

Richards, D. 1991. *Birds of Kenya – A Celebration.* Hamish Hamilton, London.

Williams, J.G. & Arlot, N. 1980 *A Field Guide to the Birds of East Africa.* Collins, London.

Index to common names